D1602956

Louise

Louise Klassen Matson

*Louise Klassen Matson's
flight to freedom
as told to*

Margaret J. Anderson

Margaret J. Anderson

*Harold Shaw Publishers
Wheaton, Illinois 60187*

The author gratefully wishes to make the following acknowledgements:
To David Hostetler, Heinrich Thielman, George Klassen,
Nick Friesen, Peter Funk, Rudy Wiebe, Margaretha Friesen,
Louise Klassen Matson and others for suggestions and the loan of
resource material that aided me in writing this book.
To residents of Reedley, Dinuba and Fresno, California,
who shared similar experiences.
To John Bergmann, travel guide, who provided information
regarding his involvement in the Amur River escape adventure.
To Rev. J. B. Toews and others who read the manuscript
to verify its historical data.

Second Printing, September 1977

Library of Congress Catalog Card Number 77-71626
ISBN 0-87788-517-6

Printed in the United States of America

Contents

Foreword

Repeatedly, in missionary deputation work, I have told the story about my family's hazardous escape from Russia through Harbin, China to escape Soviet persecution, possible imprisonment and death. Without fail those who heard the story expressed a desire to see it in print.

Since I am not a writer, I was delighted when Margaret J. Anderson consented to research historical facts and write a book about my family's flight to freedom in the United States.

Choosing to write in the first person, she steps into my shoes and relates the story as I and members of my family experienced it.

My prayer is that God may be glorified through its telling and that readers will learn to appreciate anew what it means to live in a country where we can freely worship the Lord Jesus Christ, whom we love and serve.

Louise Klassen Matson

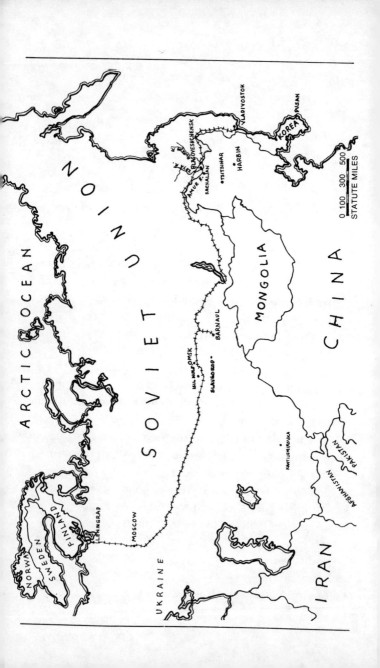

One
Danger

"Louise! Louise!"

The words had the effect of a rifle shot awakening me from a frightening, recurrent dream in which I stood, my hand tied to my brother's, so near the brink of a gaping, recently-excavated grave that I could feel the earth crumbling beneath my bare toes. Behind us Russian prison guards stood at attention, guns poised for instant triggering.

"Louise!"

A gun exploded.

"Louise!"

Feeling pain, I grabbed my shoulder. It was my mother shaking me, our toddler Nellie in her arms. I sat upright in bed and threw back the covers.

Mother turned her attention to my brother.

"George! Quick now, the cannons! They are near."

And we were ready. With careful foresight our widowed mother had prepared us for such an eventuality. Fully clothed, having been advised not to undress at bedtime for fear of the guns, we needed little urging to get moving. I ran to the window. Trembling, I watched the bursting bombs light the distant sky.

"Louise, do not dawdle."

George, older by three years than I, took my hand as together we followed Mother through the back door, stumbling across a span of pasture to the shelter of clumps of friendly birch trees. We flung ourselves on the ground, buried our heads in our arms and waited, listening.

Louder... louder... Were the planes headed toward us? We could not tell.

Suddenly the bombing ceased and the roar of the motors lessened as they receded. A ruse? A reprieve? We had no way of knowing.

I lifted my head.

"Down!" Mother hissed.

Obeying, I dropped my head in my arms, but I would not remain silent. "Mama, you said God would protect us," I whispered. "We prayed—and now the planes come at us."

"God will protect us, Louise. We must trust him."

As Mennonite children we were never encouraged to express our thoughts. Often I wondered if we were even supposed to think. But small as I was, I did plenty of thinking. How *could* we trust God? How could we be *sure* the planes would not return.?

After what seemed an eternity we crept back into the house, sleep dissipated. My mind was turning cartwheels.

I shuddered as I recalled the dramatic details of my recurring dream. Though varied in detail and substance, the gaping, recently excavated grave remained intact. Apparently my subconscious mind refused to be released from the horrors I had seen and heard.

Though the post-revolutionary Civil War had raged in Western Russia, particularly in the Ukraine, for some time, we Mennonites were just beginning to feel the effects of the Red Army infiltration into the fertile area of Western Siberia where our families were farmers.

Absurd rules and regulations were imposed upon us. One day we received a message from an aunt, Tante Agnes, Mother's half-sister, telling us that her husband had rashly disobeyed a rule imposed upon the inhabitants of their city, Isil Kulj, two miles away. No one was allowed to step off his property without permission from Russian authorities.

"And for what reason?" Uncle wanted to know. "They should tell us why not."

Since they hadn't, Uncle stepped beyond his

property line. Immediately Russian soldiers arrested and jailed him.

"I saw them grab him, but I don't know where they took him," my aunt's message informed us. "Please come and help us find him."

Grandfather harnessed a horse to a sled and he and Grandmother hastened to Isil Kulj. Upon arrival, Grandfather was also thrown into prison. Grandmother was free to return to her home until the off-limit regulations were lifted. Relatives went to fetch her and, at her insistence, they also brought my aunt and her children home to live with her. At the prison, relatives were told they would be required to provide food for their imprisoned kin.

Though food was scarce, everyone rallied to the support of the prisoners. I was only six years old at the time, but occasionally I was permitted to ride with the folks who visited Uncle and Grandfather.

"Talk only Russian when the guards are present," Mother warned. "Otherwise the men will be punished."

Not permitted to enter the prison, I recall how George and I stood at the door stamping our feet and swinging our arms to keep warm while we waited in the winter wind and snow until the visit was over.

I gasped when I peeked in and saw Grandfather's large cell block. I beckoned Grandfather to come close to the window. "Where do you sleep?" I asked. "I don't see any beds."

He pointed to a wide foot-high platform that

filled a large portion of the room. "That is our bed."

"But there are no blankets, Groszpapa. There are no mattresses. How do you keep warm?"

"We snuggle close," Grandfather answered trying to make a joke of it. But his sad smile told me that he didn't think any better of the sleeping arrangements than I.

On one visit Mother managed to converse with Grandfather alone. The story he related gave us apprehensive insight into the brutal character of the Russian prison.

"Sometimes at night," he said, "guards come through the barracks. They awaken every third person, give him a pick and shovel and order him out into the cold."

"For what?" Mother wanted to know.

Grandfather pressed a shaking finger against his lips. "Sssh! We do not know. We can only guess."

Later we learned the secret of the night disappearances. Equipped with picks and shovels, prisoners were forced to excavate mammoth graves, large enough to accommodate 40 bodies. Then they were lined up and asked to make a choice—either they could accept Communism and renounce their faith in God and live, or refuse to acquiesce to such an alternative, and die.

Prisoners who remained true to their faith were tied together, one to another, on the edge of the grave and facing it. On command they were executed. Toppling forward into the communal grave they were left to die. The next morning another contingent of prisoners was rounded up, given picks and shovels and ordered to close the grave.

One night one of the prisoners did not die. Though badly wounded, he managed to break his bonds, crawl out of the grave and escape. It was from him, via an "underground grapevine" that we learned the brutal story.

Worried relatives gathered to pray for our loved ones. "Dear God, spare the men. Let your guardian angels watch over them."

In spite of our prayers Uncle disappeared one night. When relatives arrived to deliver his food, they were turned away. "He is gone," the soldiers said.

To a concentration camp in northern Siberia? To his death in a communal grave? We never found out.

Six weeks later Grandfather was released. Apparently he had been able to convince his captors that he hadn't known the off-limit ruling applied to people outside of the city. This didn't mean we weren't terrorized thereafter, however.

A particularly harrowing experience occurred one day when I saw a horse-drawn wagon passing Ljubimovka, the close-knit family farm settlement, where we lived. Speedily, home after home emptied as people closed in to see what it contained.

"Oh, my Lord!" someone screamed. Men shook their heads sadly. Women hid their faces in their aprons and moaned.

"Stay," mother called when she saw me head for the scene.

A perverse child, a *no* command meant *go*, to me. Circumventing the crowd, I pushed my way to the wagon. I soon wished I hadn't. On it lay a dead man, partially severed fingers dangling from outstretched hands. I realized at once that, like others I had heard about, this man had been tortured and killed because he refused to renounce his faith. Relatives had claimed his body for burial.

These were difficult days for everyone, especially for a widow with three children.

Mother ripped and remade our clothing. She unraveled all the crocheted items she could find and used the thread to mend and to sew together the garments she renovated. Carefully she removed buttons and hooks-and-eyes from worn clothing and sewed them onto pieces of cardboard. She churned butter and made cottage cheese. These items George peddled in nearby Isil Kulj.

Kerosene was scarce, if not impossible to buy. So Mother made do with a cloth wick in a holder fastened to a saucer filled with sun-flower seed oil.

Forced to share our food with itinerant soldiers who banged on our door demanding meals and a few hours of rest in exchange for our safety, we often went hungry. But through it all Mother remained fearless and uncomplaining. At least that is what I thought.

One day, racing to the outhouse intent on reaching it before my brother did, I stopped short, suddenly realizing it was occupied. Someone was crying. It was Mother, crying her heart out to God

15

in dreadful sobs. Frightened, George and I pounded on the door. "Mama, why do you cry? Are you afraid? Don't you believe God will take care of us?"

Mother bit her lip, dried her tears and turned into a stoic parent once more. "Sometimes it helps to cry," was all she said.

So, I mused, grownups are also frightened. True, they tried to hide their fear as Mother did. Causes for alarm were never spelled out in so many words when we children were around. But by putting bits and pieces of conversations together we were able to learn a little of what was happening in our area and elsewhere in Russia, particularly in the Ukraine where we had lived previously.

Conversations were overheard with references to arrests, confiscation of property, murder, rape, and starvation.

Previously our people had said, "They won't bother us here." Now they weren't so sure. Had Uncle and Grandfather been arrested without a just cause?

"Doesn't God love us, Mama?" I often asked.

"God is love," she always told me. "It is men who are evil. We must trust God and be true to Him always as our forefathers were." She hesitated, suddenly in a reflective mood. "You want I should tell you about my people?"

"Yes, Mama," I answered, longing to be reminded of the good times we enjoyed before my father died. "And tell me again how Papa found you."

16

Two

My Family Tree

Where I was interested in the immediate past, Mother often spoke of long-ago events as they pertained to our people—even when I was young, though I failed to understand much of what she said at the time. She, like other parents, constantly declared that we were Hollanders, not Germans or Russians. Yet, we spoke German as well as Dutch and we lived in Russia.

"Our ancestors were born in Holland," she told me. "Like us, they believed only people who are sorry for their sins and take Jesus to be their Lord and master should be baptized and join the church.

"They were pacifists who believed it was more important to obey God than man or a government that wanted them to fight in wars. Because of their beliefs they were badly persecuted.''

"What does *persecuted* mean?" I asked.

"Much trouble. During the reign of the Holy Roman Emperor, Charles V, many of these people joined the church organized by a converted priest, Menno Simons. Because they were considered rebels they were tied to poles and burned. Some had their hands tied behind their backs and were drowned. Some were torn apart."

I shuddered. "Didn't they cry for help?"

"The men who arrested them stuffed rags or apples in their mouths to keep them from praising God when they died."

"Why didn't they move away?"

"They did. To a place that later became known as Prussia. There, under the rule of Frederick the Great, they built dykes and drained and reclaimed the marsh lands of the Vistula Valley."

"Could they worship the way they wanted?"

"For a good many years, yes. It is a long story. . . ." And one that Mother wasn't able always to remember in detail. Frederick the Great had granted the Mennonites religious freedom and, as an inducement to move to Prussia, promised they would not have to pay taxes or fight in the army.

In time, however, some of his countrymen forced him to require the Mennonites to pay taxes to support the army.

Frederick's successor increased the military tax and demanded that children born to mixed marriages, Prussian and Mennonites, serve in the army. He also refused them permission to purchase more land when their children married and wished to establish farms of their own.

About that time, Catherine the Great won a great deal of land along the Black and Caspian Seas from the Turks. Hoping to rehabilitate the land, she invited Europeans to settle in the area. She promised them wood for their homes and gave each family 500 rubles if they accepted her invitation.

Many Mennonites responded to her invitation. A special charter drawn up in 1788, (and later reaffirmed by Tsar Paul I in 1800) granted these settlers religious freedom, non-interference in education and civic affairs and immunity from military involvement. They were forbidden, however, to propagandize their religious beliefs.

The first emigrants settled on the banks of the Choritza River, a tributary of the Dneiper. Life was not easy for them, however. Disease and death took a heavy toll. Rains damaged their temporary dwellings. Wood for housing didn't arrive when promised and when it did come, much of it was of poor quality. Yet, by the turn of the century, 400 families had established fifteen villages in what came to be known as the *Choritza* or the *Old Colony*.

In spite of hardships suffered by the early settlers, the Mennonites continued their emigration. By 1859 three other colonies, the *Molotschna*, near the Molotschnaya River, and the *Am Trakt* and the *Alexandertal*, near the Volga, had been established.

My mother, Margaretha Funk, the oldest of four children, was born in a small village, Freedensfelt, in the *Alexandertal Colony*.

Much alike architecturally, oblong and box-like, the early homes were built in close proximity, of brick and adobe to protect them from fire.

The gable ends of Grandfather Funk's home faced the street. The front door faced a private driveway on one side of the house. Windows were shuttered to keep out heat in summer and cold in winter.

A grove of birches, the corral and the orchard lay behind the house. A lover of nature, Grandfather planted flowers and even a few fruit trees in his front yard which he separated from the street with a white brick fence.

Since each village enjoyed local autonomy, citizens established their own schools, churches, and medical facilities (usually a cooperative endeavor of several settlements). In Russia, Mennonite young men were allowed to work in the forestry or the medical corps in lieu of army service.

In the forestry service they planted, cultivated and protected Russian forests. Away from home for four years, they depended on home villages to house, feed and clothe them while they were away. Those associated with the medical corps worked in hospitals or on army detail.

Though some churches were larger than others, they were for the most part plain, oblong buildings. The pulpit stood on a platform built along one side

of the church. The *vorsänger* (music director) took
his pitch from a special tuning fork. Since song books
were scarce, hymns were sung by rote. The *vorsänger* sang a phrase: "Come, Holy Spirit...."
and the congregation would echo the words,
"Come, Holy Spirit..,." Then he would sing the
next phrase, "Heavenly Dove," and the remaining
phrases, which the congregation repeated until the
hymn was concluded.

Fraternizing between sexes was unheard of in
church. The men always sat on one side, the women
on the other.

In Mother's village school, sessions were held in
the largest, roomiest home. Students studied around
a long wooden table, boys on one side, girls on the
other, the teacher at the end of the table.

Like most Mennonite girls, Mother remained in
school for a very brief period of time. Homemaking
skills provided all the status she required.

It was into this culture that Mother, at the age of
17, learned the subtleties of a Mennonite romance.
She was always eager to respond to my request that
she tell me how Papa "found" her.

"One day an Uncle from a nearby village came to
visit us," Mother recounted. " 'Margaretha, do you
have a picture of yourself?' he wanted to know."

" 'Yaj, why do you ask?'

" 'I think perhaps your cousin would like to have
it.'

"*A picture of me*! I was surprised. *Why should
anyone want a picture of me*, I thought. 'I will get

21

it for you', I told him. So I gave Uncle my picture.

"I forgot all about it until one day a tall, skinny school teacher came to visit our home. It was then my papa told me that he had received a letter from this man. He had asked Uncle to get the picture for him. He liked me. So he asked Papa if he could marry me. Papa questioned him about his love for Jesus and about his work as a school teacher. Then he decided he was a good man for me.

"So after he courted me for two months, we were married." Mother smiled warmly as she often did when she spoke of this Cornelius Klassen who was destined to become my father. "Together we set up housekeeping in a teacherage in Kantijemirovka. There your brother George was born... such a good boy...."

I knew what she meant. George was as unlike me as a mild breeze is unlike a gusty wind.

"Then three years later you were born," Mother told me. Papa was glad to get a girl. Next was Abraham, who died during the scarlet fever/whooping cough epidemic. You were very sick but you did not die, even though you said '*Nein*' when we tried to give you your medicine. A neighbor lady tried to bribe you. 'A lump of sugar? Just take your medicine....' But you would not take it. When she tried to pry your mouth open you bit her hand." Mother shook her head. "But George took his medicine. No complaining. Louise, sometimes I think you were born with your fists clenched."

Mother spoke from experience. She knew my

stubborn nature. If we were spanked for some wrongdoing, George took his punishment without a whimper. "I deserved it," he'd tell me. "I cry only when I haven't done anything bad." Even then he soft-pedaled his crying. I? I yelled so the entire village heard me. To prove I was innocent? More likely to frighten Mother into lessening the punishment.

Shortly before I was born, many of our relatives, responding to a "lots-of-land/lots-of-space enticement," migrated eastward to the rich Western Siberian plains where they received without cost or for a nominal sum, land needed for expansion. There, in the vicinity of Omsk, they helped establish the large *Slavgorod/Barnaul Colony*. Being a teacher, not a farmer, my father remained behind.

Though we missed our relatives we were not unhappy. Father, who had been educated in a teachers' college at Halbstad, was a kind, easy-going man who cherished every moment he had with us children. Often he joggled me on his knee as he sang:

Schushe, patrushe, vaut rushlet em stroh?
(Hush, hush, what rustles in the straw?)

De janskies gone boast en kabe kene shoh.
(The geese are going barefoot and have no shoes.)

De shuste hafta lada, oba kene laste doato.
(The shoemaker has leather, but no lasts for
    them.)

23

Schushe, patrushe, vaut rushlet em stroh?
(Hush, hush, what rustles in the straw?)

I recall how warm and greatly loved I felt as I snuggled in his arms. At other times he concocted stories which he told to George and me. I especially enjoyed it when he tucked me in bed and listened to my prayers. A favorite:

Ich bin Klein, mein herz ist rein,
(I am small, my heart is clean,)

Soll neimand drinn wohnen, also Jesus allein!
    Amen.
(No one will live in it but Jesus alone! Amen.)

Throughout my childhood I was convinced that his and Mother's marriage wasn't arranged by my grandparents as much as by God. Perhaps I have forgotten, but I cannot recall that he ever spoke a demanding, unkind word to Mother.

One day, as if driven by overwhelming apprehension and fear, Father announced that he had decided to join our relatives in their closely knit village, Ljubimovka, in Western Siberia.

"But why?" Mother wanted to know. "You are a teacher. You said you would never become a farmer."

"Soon there will be much trouble in the Ukraine," Father answered. "We should move now before it is too late."

He was right. Our move preceded by only a few months the Bolshevist Revolution and the Civil War between the White (non-Communist) and the Red (Communist) Armies that followed.

In Russia one doesn't run away from the consequences of such an upheaval, however. We, too, were doomed to suffer from them.

Three
A World of Change

How much do I, an adult, remember of the sudden move across the country at the age of three? Very little, it seems. Yet memories and impressions stored deep in my subconscious do surface at times —among them the fear of loss when seeing all our belongings packed into barrels and, together with our furniture, loaded onto freight cars.

"Papa, look! They're taking our things!"

"I know. They will be in Ljubimovka when we get there," he told me.

"My doll?" I wondered if I'd ever see my tattered treasure again.

"Your doll, too. It is in one of the barrels."

There are memories, too, of the happiness we felt

because soon we would be reunited with grand-parents, aunts, uncles, and cousins. By now well established on farms in Western Siberia, they had extolled the rich soil and the abundant yields of grain, vegetables and fruit so well that they persuaded my teacher-at-heart father to escape impending trials and try farming.

I can still *feel* the bouncy, seemingly endless ride on a train which was more boxcar than coach, with bench-like shelves along the sides to serve as seats by day, as berths by night . . . restlessness and boredom . . . and the proverbial questions: "How much longer? When will we get there?"

Eventually we did arrive in Ljubimovka where Father had purchased a house on the same street and about 200 yards from Grandfather Funk's roomy home. We rejoiced at seeing our family again, especially Uncle John Funk, Mother's brother, Tante Suse and Cousin Peter who lived near us.

Everyone talked at once, recounting all the events that had happened since last we met. We children visited all of the homes and explored the orchards and the groves of birch trees which stood, like tall straight sentinels behind our home. Most exciting to George and me was the arrival of our baby sister, Nellie, a few months later. Like a beautiful china doll, she seemed too fragile to touch. Yet Mother let me caress her, and on occasion, even allowed me to hold her. "You must be careful not to drop her," Mother would tell me when I'd crawl up into the rocking chair so she could put little Nellie in my arms.

Because Father had always loved teaching, he felt a great loss when he watched the village youngsters skipping down the street on their way to school when it opened the first fall we lived in Ljubimovka.

"You miss the children?" Mother asked.

"I didn't know I would miss teaching so much," he answered. "But I know it is best we are here. And, Margaretha, I want to tell you that I have made a decision. I am going to study to be a minister. I can farm *and* be a minister."

Mother grabbed his hands and squeezed them. "I am glad," she said. She felt somewhat responsible for his having decided to move to Ljubimovka, at least that is what she informed the relatives. "In Kantijemirovka I often spoke of loneliness for the family."

"Surely God is good," my parents often told us, as they thanked him for his guidance and care. Before long, however, apprehension began to creep into their prayers. When relatives gathered, they spoke of Communist suppression and terror. It wasn't until much later that we understood what these words meant, or the reality behind the words.

Soon after the war broke out in Europe in 1914, influential newspapers in Russia initiated a hate campaign against all Germans. Incriminating articles labeled all Germans as spies, enemies of the state.

At first we Mennonites escaped some of this heat due largely to the praiseworthy work of the Sanitäter (hospital workers). During the war six thousand of these men worked in hospitals and with army ambulance corps. Eventually, however, we too became targets of discrimination.

When Lenin began his rule, he demanded that all land, livestock and implements owned by the Crown, the churches, wealthy landlords and monastaries be transfered, without any compensation, to the state.

This action caused dissent and rebellion which in turn led to the Civil War fought between the Red and the White (united opposition groups) armies. Though fighting took place on many fronts, it centered in the Ukraine where the battle front shifted back and forth across Mennonite territory twenty-three times. A vast number of our people were killed and many villages completely destroyed.

I recall hearing an aunt say, "The women and girls! So many raped!" Though I had no idea what it meant to be raped, I could tell by her distress that she thought death would be more tolerable.

Historians say that Mennonites by the thousands died as a result of the war, the famine and the typhus epidemic that followed it. When the Civil War moved into our area of Western Siberia so did typhus. Two years after we settled in Ljubimovka, Father came down with typhoid fever.

One evening he and George hitched the horses to a wagon and set out to deliver grain to a distant feed mill. Arriving at their destination they found many other farmers waiting in line to unload their sacks of grain. When darkness fell everyone bedded down for the night right there, spreading blankets they had brought with them onto already unloaded sacks of grain.

The next morning, when Father unloaded his wagon, it began to rain, hard. He and George were soaked to the skin by the time they reached home.

Mother insisted that they change clothes immediately. Father demurred, "I am desperately weary. I did not sleep well last night. Let me lie down and rest for just a few minutes."

While he was resting Mother helped George get into dry clothing. To her dismay she found lice in his wet clothing, no doubt picked up from his sleeping companions. When she wakened Father to help him change he said he felt feverish. We know now that the lice he and George had picked up were typhus carriers. Though George was not affected by them, within hours Father became desperately ill.

Frantic, we did what all good Mennonites do. We prayed. Mother told God it would be impossible for her to live without someone to provide for her children. Kneeling beside my mother I clenched my fists and cried, "God, you can't let Papa die! He's going to be a minister. Don't you know he has already bought his striped pants and long swallow-tail minister coat?"

But he did die, and I blamed God for our misfortune.

One of my uncles, assisted by an escaped Austrian prisoner of war whom my parents had befriended and permitted to work for us, built my father's coffin—a wooden box with a glass window in the lid so the body could be viewed even after it was sealed (an epidemic precaution).

When we begged Mother to let us see him, she hesitated. "I do not think. . . ."

"Please!"

"Go quickly then. George, take care of Louise."

George took my hand and together we tiptoed to the shed where Father lay in state. I had to stand on my toes to peer through the viewing glass.

I gasped. That wasn't our Father lying there wrapped in a white sheet. It couldn't be. So thin: so pale! I turned and ran to Mother who gathered me in her arms and wept as she tried to comfort me.

The funeral, delayed as long as possible because of unseasonably persistent rainfall, was held in Grandfather's home, which was the largest in the community.

Again as a protective measure, the coffin was not brought into the home. It remained in the rain where it had been placed on a wagon hearse in the street in front of the home.

I recall standing by the window watching the steady plop, plop of the rain on the casket, screaming at the top of my lungs, "I want Papa! I want Papa!" My five-year old mind couldn't comprehend what had happened to us. Why didn't they bring him in out of the rain? Why didn't God listen to our prayers? Didn't he have ears? Didn't he care that Father could no longer joggle us children on his knee or listen to our bedtime prayers?

Six of my uncles rode with the body to the cemetery where it was lowered into a watery, rain-filled grave. I stuffed my fingers into my ears when my uncles related what had happened. I wished I had done so sooner. Not to know would have been better. . . .

I had always feared death. I hated it when a pet or one of the farm animals died. Now I shuddered every time I thought about it. And for years falling rain was horrifying to me. I remember often asking God to let me die on a bright sunny day.

What does a mother, the wife of a farmer, do when left alone with three small children after her husband dies? In our case, she turned to her kin. They helped her plant crops and assisted her with the harvesting. My brother, George, now nine, assumed more and more chore responsibilities.

And I started school. Rebelliously, I'll have to admit.

"Are you ready, Louise?" Mother asked, when school opened.

I shook my head. "I'm not going," I told her.

"And why, I ask?"

"Because I'm too dumb. I've got to learn something first."

Mother prevailed, however, and I went off to school to learn the somethings I didn't know.

A year later, the undeserved arrests of my uncle and grandfather triggered the recurrent nightmare dream of imprisonment and execution that haunted my sleep.

It was during this time, too, that the Communist regime imposed a system of mandatory sharing of all farm produce to help feed the establishment and the Red Army. Farmers were forced to pay a stiff grain tax. The result: little grain for seed, little flour for bread. Before long one of the world's worst famines swept across the land. Starvation became a ghost that everyone feared.

Visits by soldiers grew more frequent. Always during daytime hours, there was a scurrying of feet when we heard them approach. Quickly the prisoner of war must disappear into the hiding place prepared in the barn. Now pile the straw high against the opening. Quick! At night we fled to the birch grove.

"Why do you give these men our food?" George asked Mother one day after she had fed two of the soldiers.

Grabbing her shoulders Mother folded her arms tightly across her breasts. "So I . . . so we will not be harmed," she said. "Someday you will understand. Besides they would take it anyway."

In spite of shortages Mother made do with what she had. She also sold whatever she thought we could spare. It was during this time that she sent George into the nearby village to peddle the snaps, hooks and eyes which she had removed from old clothing, as well as home-churned butter and cottage cheese.

Other children sold similar items. I recall how these junior salesmen gathered together after each trip to compare payment they had received for their merchandise. One cousin was chastised mercilessly for underselling the others.

I recall, too, that Mother herself often refrained from eating when we did.

"Why don't you eat, Mama?" we would ask.

"Mama is not hungry today," she would answer.

Concern for her half-sister, Anna Friesen, bed-ridden with a stroke and suffering recurrent attacks, added to her worries. Since it was taken for granted she would not live, Mother sorrowed for her. And, as is customary anywhere, the relatives speculated about the consequences of her death.

Children are meant to be seen and not heard. I learned it is sometimes worse to hear than to be seen. I hadn't meant to eavesdrop. The aunts in our settlement didn't know I was within listening distance.

"Did you know Anna has asked John to marry Margaretha when she dies?"

"No! What would she do with all those children?"

"She needs someone to take care of her. . . ."

"Anna thinks she would make a better wife than some young girl. She has asked John to marry Margaretha."

"John would be lucky."

Stop it! I wanted to shout as I crept away, refusing to believe what I heard.

Aunt Anna's husband, John Friesen, owned a large fine house in Alexanderkron, thirty miles away. But to move from Lujbimovka where all

Mother's relatives lived? No! And have this Uncle John take Father's place in our home. Unthinkable! It wasn't true, it couldn't be.

"Say *no*, Mama," I pleaded when I told her what I had heard.

"Louise, Louise, you worry too much. Maybe Anna won't die. She could get better. You can pray that she gets better."

That I would not do. Hadn't I prayed that Father would get better and he died. Maybe if I didn't pray at all she would live.

But, like Father, she did die.

No longer were rumors of marriage spoken secretly. Speculations were voiced openly.

"Will Margaretha marry John?"

"She would have a fine home...."

"What can a woman do without a man?"

"John's strong. He can stand up to anyone."

"You can say that again...."

four
We Get A New Father

My mother, Margaretha Klassen, and her brother-in-law, John Friesen, were married on June 2, 1921, two months after her half-sister's death. The wedding took place in Grandfather Funk's home.

In that interim I had come to accept the idea of a new husband for Mama, a new father for George, Nellie and me. In fact, I looked forward to the wedding. Mother, George, Nellie and I would be living in Uncle John Friesen's fine home, with older brothers who would do all the chores!

Though I had attended very few weddings I thought of them as happy affairs. I recall the times we children acted out weddings of our own. On one occasion Cousin Peter was the minister. I was the bride! Cousin Hans, the groom.

"I need a Bible," Peter said.

"You can use Groszpapa's," Hans answered.

Peter whistled. "In the orchard?"

"And why not?" I asked. "I will get it."

Peter propped the Bible on a stump of one of the fruit trees. Then he asked Hans and me to step forward to be married. He sounded so solemn I began to giggle. Hans punched me in the ribs.

"Will you take....?"

Choking with laughter, I answered, "I will." Slowpoke Hans took his time. "I will!" he said, striking fist in the palm of his hand.

Since we couldn't remember just how a wedding should end, we simply pinched each other and Peter pronounced us husband and wife.

Our elders considered our play wedding sacreligious. They scolded us for sneaking Grandfather's big Bible into the orchard. Unforgivable! And a wedding yet! "For shame! Don't you know marriage is serious business?"

Of course, but now at Mother's wedding it seemed everyone acted much *too* serious. I couldn't understand why. Everyone crying? Were they remembering Father's funeral in the same home two years before? They should forget. They should be glad Mother was getting a husband to help take care of her children.

Following a lengthy sermon by our pastor, Mother in her Sunday dress, and her stocky husband-to-be with his dark mustache, imperial goatee and his black Sunday suit, stood for the marriage ritual.

"Will you take this man to be your wedded husband?" the pastor intoned.

Warily Mother glanced at her children *and* at the brood who would become hers. Then, as if bracing herself for the inevitable, she stood tall and answered firmly: "Ja, I will."

Her answer changed the mood of the occasion. I thought I heard a corporate sigh as everyone relaxed.

After the ceremony coffee and zwieback were served as all the guests visited together. Then, as we went to our respective homes, our new father came home with us. The next day we moved to his home in Alexanderkron.

I was as impressed by his pretentious home as I had been the times we had visited it before. The largest and finest in the village, it had brick center-wall ovens to keep us warm, calcimined summer and winter kitchens, bedrooms, dining, living and sitting rooms with board ceilings that I remembered Aunt Anna saying had to be scrubbed clean once a year.

I walked through the rooms scarcely daring to breathe. This was my new home. What would it be like to live here? The dining room contained few pieces of furniture—a buffet, a clothes cabinet, a long wooden table with benches on both sides and a chair at each end. So many dishes in the buffet! I opened the closet door. Some of Aunt Anna's clothes still hung there. They would have to go to make room for Mother's.

I sat down on one of the benches mentally seating the members of our new family. Uncle John would sit at one end, I was sure, and Mother at the other. I wondered if I would ever be able to call Uncle John *Papa*. To me he was my uncle. Perhaps I should call him Mr. Friesen. Some of the Mennonite women called their husbands by their last name. "It is because they honor them," Mother explained. "The man, he is the head of the house." I was sure Uncle John would be the head of the house. That settled it. I would call him Mr. Friesen—at least to myself.

On one wall hung a picture of Lenin, the revolutionist dictator we had come to fear and hate.

When George saw it he gasped. "He is not our leader," he said.

"But he is our ruler. And God says we should pray for those who rule over us," my step-father countered. And we did, every day during family devotions. We prayed that he would become the kind of leader we believed he should be. We prayed, too, that he would somehow choose Christ as his Lord and Savior.

When I mustered enough courage I entered the living room (which I had been told was used only when company called). I wanted to sit down and try to play the organ but I didn't dare. Instead I sat on the sofa and read the framed embroidered Scripture mottoes "Herre auf Gott" "Halte fest was du hast, das niemand deine Krone nehme."

Nearby, yet a short distance away from the

house, stood a tool shed. At one end was a grind-stone used to grind wheat into flour; at the other end was an apartment to house hired men when they worked on the farm. Behind the house, and con-nected to it by a small passageway, was the building that housed the animals. George and I thought, "Such grand horses and so many cows!"

Always in command, Mr. Friesen put us to work immediately. "Louise, you can begin in the straw-berry patch. Come, I will show you...."

"Like this." He knelt and began to remove the plant runners. "Do you think you can do this?" he asked.

I stood tall and tossed my dark braids indignantly. "I can," I answered.

I didn't feel so confident a few hours later. I began to hate my back-breaking job. Now I wasn't sure it had been wise for Mother to marry again. For one thing we had to get used to thinking of our cousins as brothers and sisters. In adjusting to each other, life didn't always work out as smoothly as we wished.

My mother, my step-father and Nick, his young-est son, shared one bedroom. Nellie and I moved into Anna's bedroom (by this time Liese, the older daughter, had married and moved to a home of her own). Anna made room for us reluctantly. I didn't blame her. How nice it would be, I thought, to have a room all to oneself. The three boys, Henry, John and Abe rearranged their bedrom so George and Henry Loewen, a cousin from the Ukraine who had

41

been living with us for some time, could move in with them. So crowded!

At one time the Friesen family ate very well. Now, however, we lived in a belt-tightening, make-do or do-without era. Breakfast consisted chiefly of bread and butter (actually a butter-substitute: the speckled bottom layer of rendered lard mixed with salt) and coffee made from rye grains which, after being threshed, were cooked in buttermilk, dried, roasted and hand ground before being prepared for a meal. Sometimes fried potatoes and cracklings (the crisp pork rind from which lard had been rendered) were also served at breakfast, especially to the menfolk. Cracklings were good. I often sneaked some when Mother wasn't looking.

At dinner, our noon meal, we ate cabbage borsch, boiled potatoes, fried eggs or homemade noodles and gravy. On rare occasions meat was combined with the noodles. At supper we were fed fried potatoes, boiled eggs, bread and milk.

As time passed, obtaining grain for flour became a serious problem, especially for the large—the "expert" farmers as the Russians called them, who were required to part with an additional grain tax after the first had been paid. In such cases farmers were robbed not only of flour for bread but of grain for spring planting as well.

Ingeniously Mr. Friesen thought of a plan to outwit the government officials. He removed the floor boards in the garret space above our rooms. Then he poured wheat and rye into the troughs between the risers and replaced the boards. When we needed flour, he removed a board, took out the specified amount of grain and brought it out to the tool shed and ground it into flour. Always he had to be careful not to deplete the supply needed to plant his spring crop.

When officials called to see if he had given as much grain as they believed he should, they were shown the empty bins in the barn.

Eventually conditions became so bad that many malnourished people died of cholera. I don't know what would have happened if the American Red Cross hadn't come to our aid and provided rice for needy families.

Besides becoming our father when he married Mother, Mr. Friesen also became our dentist. One day George complained of a toothache. After investigating, my step-father decided the tooth should be pulled. "Sit down," he told George. "John, you hold his head so he does not move. Now, open...." George opened his mouth and in what seemed only a second Mr. Friesen extracted the tooth.

Fortunately I had few tooth problems. This may have been due to the fact that I was constantly admonished. "Eat your crusts, then you will have strong teeth." But more likely, it was the niggardly use of sugar in our home which accounted for my sound teeth. Periodically our village received a 25 pound sugar allotment (in a block like rock salt). It was chipped into smaller portions for use in cooking and baking. I recall how we children sat on the floor, mouths watering, scrounging for chips that might fly our way. If one of the women suspected we had picked up too generous a portion she would say, "Open your hand." Often she added, "Too big. Return to table."

I came to know what it meant to be jealous in those days. I was especially jealous of Nick. I was sure he feigned illness far too frequently to gain Mother's attention and sympathy. Now I realize it was only natural that he should resent Nellie replacing him as the baby in the home. And she was a baby, a true "mama's" baby. But who could blame her? She, too, had to fight for attention and love.

I was also jealous of Anna whose hand-me-down clothing I inherited. Not that this practice was uncommon in Mennonite homes. The problem: Anna was short, I taller and, at that time, skinny. And among Mennonite girls it was not proper to wear short dresses.

"Where are you, God?" I often asked, feeling he really wasn't concerned about all the problems I faced. Mother had told me he could live in my heart. I knew that, but I did nothing about inviting him in.

Oh, I made an attempt to live for him for a brief period of time. Once when special meetings were held in our home I was convicted of continually rebelling against the discipline under which I lived. When the meeting concluded with an invitation to repentance I looked around for Nick, who, even though I was jealous of him, was really a very close friend as well as brother. He had slipped out of the meeting. I found him in his room crying. "I am a sinner, I need Jesus," he sobbed.

"I am worse," I told him. "Come with me."

Together we made our way back to the living room. There we knelt and asked God to forgive our sins.

It's one thing to make a commitment, it's another thing to live it. For Nick and me it seemed impossible. Any small infraction was condemned as un-Christian by the older children who cared little about God. "And you think you are Christian? Why don't you act like one?"

When they were asked to tend to a particular chore they smiled smugly. "Nick and Louise will be glad to do it. They are Christians now."

Because our parents were Christians I believed what we did in our home should reflect their faith. Yet, when they left home for a trip to Omsk or a visit with relatives, the older boys invited friends over for a card party. From somewhere they produced vodka which they consumed in generous quantities.

When my parents returned I felt obligated to confess the boys' sins to them. Angry, the boys vowed they'd get even with me. The next time the folks visited elsewhere I was bent over a table and given a good beating. "Promise you will never tell on us again? Promise?"

I had no choice. I promised. Yet, I tattled time and time again. And just as repeatedly I was punished by the boys. I prayed to God to make them stop. He didn't. So I decided it would be easier not to be a Christian.

George, who remembered our first father better than I, didn't believe our new father loved Mother as he should. "When I get big and marry," he said, "I'm going to kiss my wife. I'm going to hold her hand and tell her I love her." And I vowed I would do the same with my husband.

At the time neither George nor I understood that when it comes to expressing affection some people are more reserved than others. It was so with Mr. Friesen who regarded seriously his position as head of the home. His word was law. I recall that he always expected meals to be served punctually—not an easy task, especially on washdays when Mother soaked, scrubbed, boiled, rinsed and wrung (by hand) clothing, towels and bedding for our large family, or on breadmaking days when she baked loaves by the score.

It took a long time before I willingly called Uncle John Friesen, *Papa*. But when I did he seemed pleased. He took my hand in his and squeezed it, tears in his eyes. I know now that he really wanted to be our father.

Though we often complained about the older children, eventually we grew quite fond of them. I felt really lost when Henry left home at twenty-one, supposedly to work in the Forestry Corps. We learned later that he had been drafted by the military to serve as an aide for an officer who was more White than Red.

In Alexanderkron we attended school in a building constructed by the village for that purpose. My step-father's brother, a minister, taught our school and conducted village worship services which were also held in the school since we had no separate church building. Our school day always opened with an hour of Bible study and prayer.

One day our teacher, who looked and talked much like Father, informed us he had received a letter from the government officials telling him he could no longer teach the Bible. "Look," he said as he waved the Bible above his head, "I've been asked to burn this book. That I will not do. So I must resign as your teacher." He admonished us to remain true to the Book no matter what the cost.

"Remember the Bible says we should beware of people who can harm our souls. I will continue preaching even if I am killed because I do. And though you can't study the Bible in school any more, you can hide it in your hearts so you won't sin against God."

Though he continued conducting worship services in our home for some time, I don't know what happened to him eventually. I do recall, however, hearing how ministers and priests were tortured by the Communists who tried to force them to renounce their faith. One man who visited our home said he had been stabbed repeatedly and left for dead at the time his parents and sisters were killed following a midweek prayer service. He was terribly scarred.

A Communist, a short stocky man with cruel eyes, replaced our teacher. Immediately he began to ridicule the tenets of our faith and to propagandize Soviet principles. When he denied the existence of God and the creation story, some students refuted what he said even though they were severely punished for doing so.

"From now on," the new teacher informed us, "we will use the Russian language in all our speaking and studying. No more German. No more Dutch." he commanded.

Though we had been taught the Russian alphabet and could understand a great many words, and even speak a few, we found it impossible not to resort to German or Dutch when we conversed with each other. I was no more guilty than the rest but I recall being forced to kneel on hard beans until I promised I would never talk Dutch or German with my friends. One boy was stripped to his waist and viciously beaten with a yardstick because he forgot and spoke German when answering a question the teacher asked.

It was at this time that brother Abe became ill with some type of bone disease that left him severely crippled. To me it seemed that God was heaping one trial after another on our lives.

Then in 1924, after a long period of illness, Lenin died. How we rejoiced! Now life would be better. No more Communist teachers . . . no more sharing of crops. . . . That's what I and many of the other school children thought.

On Mayday that year our village honored Lenin. Carrying red Communist flags with their hammer and sickle insignia (provided by the government in a limited number) and camouflaged copies made out of red handkerchiefs we had been asked to bring from home so each student could have one, we paraded through the village, smirks on our faces, chanting (when it was safe to do so) slogans I had concocted, "Lenin is dead and we are ahead." "Lenin is dead, hurray, hurray. Now we can go back to our old way."

It has been said that children reflect the attitudes of their elders. This meant we reflected sound, strong family ties, self-reliance, desire for religious freedom and a belief that government should not interfere in personal affairs—all standards which the Communist leaders insisted must be obliterated.

Obliteration came to mean liquidation of the *kulaks*—the bourgeoisie, the wealthier land owners, as well as anyone who opposed collective principles. They were the perpetuators of these standards, according to the Communists.

Father owned much land. He owned more than one cow, more than one horse, and a threshing machine. Could he be called a *kulak*?

It wasn't long before we learned the answer to that all-important question.

five
"We Will Emigrate!"

An intense power struggle erupted within the Political Bureau, the policy making body of the Communist Party's Central Committee, following the death of Nikolai Lenin. The most prominent officials all wanted to step into the deceased dictator's shoes.

Trotsky, who ranked next to Lenin, advocated the expansion of socialism throughout Russia and the promotion of a world revolution. Nicholas Bukarin felt Lenin's policies should be continued in Russia alone, since the world wasn't ready for a revolution. Joseph Stalin believed in world-wide socialism but insisted it would succeed without a world revolution.

Cunningly Stalin managed to outwit his rivals one by one. At the Communist party Congress, in December, 1927, he won a sweeping victory to become the top man in the Politburo. The First Five-Year Plan, which he suggested should go into effect in 1928, had two major goals: nationalization of farmland into *kolkozys* (collective farms) and rapid expansion of industrial production with support from all the people.

We soon began to feel the effects of these proposals. An old Russian maxim claims that news travels faster than a bird flies. This seemed to be true when Father obtained a Fordson tractor through the Mennonite Central Committee and its affiliation with the American Relief Administration organized by Herbert Hoover. Immediately, a government official came to investigate.

All smiles and honey-tongued, he complimented Father on the wise acquisition of such a prize piece of farm equipment. "Excellent! Excellent!" he exclaimed. "Soon we will establish our *kolkhozy* here. Then you will be honored for the privilege of donating it to the cause."

Father held his tongue until the man left. Then he exploded. "Nein! That I will never do."

A few days later he attended an agriculture meeting in a neighboring community. In conversing with a group of farmers he expressed fear that the Communists would soon control all of the farms in the area.

The men laughed at him. "Friesen. you are out of

your mind."

"They hint they want my tractor."

"I heard you had one," one of the farmers answered. "You are a lucky man."

"Not if they take it from me for a *kolkhozy*," Father answered. "I would rather destroy it."

Apparently one of the men wasn't as afraid to own it as Father was, for shortly after that meeting the tractor disappeared. The village children were disappointed. They loved its belligerent roar . . . and the rides it provided.

And now it was gone, as was an ever-increasing amount of our freedom. The Communists assumed complete control of the schools, banning any kind of religious instruction. Even choral renditions of folk and religious songs were forbidden.

Christians were denied the right to assemble in their churches or in the schools (if they had been using them for that purpose, as we had). They were also told they could no longer support their charitable organizations—children's homes and hospitals.

Kulak! Word reached us that anyone so designated, either because he owned an excessive amount of property or because he failed to acquiesce to government dictates, automatically lost his citizenship rights.

In the Ukraine, thousands of Mennonites, classified as *kulaks*, were arrested, imprisoned and exiled to the far northern regions of Siberia. Condemned to a life of hard labor, they gathered pulpwood for export, built Siberian railroads and dug mines. Trainloads of Mennonites were torn from their families never to be heard from again.

With terror in our hearts we pondered anew the inevitable question, "Is Father a *kulak*?"

Henry's surprise home-coming settled the question for us. "I have been dismissed from the military," he told us. "They call me the son of a *kulak*. They tell me I am no longer a Russian citizen."

He explained how he had been grilled and how he had responded to his interrogators. Yes, his father owned several cows—he had a big family to feed. Yes, several horses. A big house and much land? Yes, and more than one change of clothing—for church on Sunday.

A few days later an official called at our home. He wanted to talk to Father alone. Later we learned he had questioned Father as the other officials had questioned Henry, most likely to verify the statements he had made.

Now there was no doubt in anyone's mind. Father was informed that he was a *kulak*, an alien, stripped of all citizenship rights. This meant he could be arrested and if not killed, at least separated from his family forever.

"We will emigrate. We will leave Russia," he said. Suddenly quiet, he looked at us children. "You must tell no one outside of the family, *no one*." His piercing black eyes singled me out. "You understand?" I nodded knowing that, of all of us, I would have the most difficulty keeping this news a secret. Repeatedly my relatives described me as one who "surely didn't fall on her mouth when she was born."

But this time there must be no telling. I understood why. We no longer knew whom we could trust. Communists had infiltrated local government councils. Code designations had been given residents so it would be easy for one farmer to inform on another.

Unknown to us, Father had already weighed the possibility of emigration. Now he took off for Omsk to try to secure passports to Canada, the country that for some time had permitted Mennonite emigration.

He came home empty handed, however, the worry lines on his face deepening. "I gave them 200 rubles," he told us. "They said *no*, come back and apply later." Since each application meant the expenditure of an additional sum of money, his repeated trips to Omsk over a period of six months became a costly venture.

Then one day the news apread like wildfire through our area, some Mennonites from the Slavgorod/Barnaul Colony had secured passports in Moscow. "I will go to Moscow," Father told us. "But, first we must sell our property ... and we must do it quickly. It is no longer safe to delay. We must also find a place where the family can live while I am away."

I'll never understand fully the compassion Grandfather and Grandmother Funk showed our family. Tante Agnes and her family had lived with them since her husband's arrest and disappearance. Now Mother's parents said, "Come and live with us. We will make room for you until you are ready to leave the country."

Within a few days cows, sheep, horses, household furnishings and farm machinery were auctioned at a public sale. We were fortunate. Shortly afterward such sales were forbidden by the government.

But none of us enjoyed that day. We said goodbye to pet cows and sheep that responded to special names we had given to them. We said goodbye, too, to horses that had served us faithfully. Father watched the proceedings stoically. Once I caught him wiping tears from his eyes, however. And one night after we had moved to Grandfather Funk's home (we all slept in the same room—Mother, Father and Abe, our crippled brother, on cots, the rest of us on the floor), I heard Father weep. But why? Doesn't he want to leave Russia? Besides, he is a man and men do not cry.

"Why does Papa cry?" I asked Mother in the morning.

"You heard?" she asked.

I nodded.

Mother hesitated, perplexed as to how to answer me. "It is hard for a man to sell everything he has worked so hard to get. It is hard to leave land and house. He feels very bad."

Tensions mounted in the weeks that followed, not so much from our crowded living conditions as from fear of what might happen to Father on what we had learned could be a disastrous trip to and from Moscow. What if he were killed . . . or arrested and exiled to northern Siberia? I'm sure we didn't understand the actual probability of such experiences until he returned to Ljubimovka, tired and dejected.

" 'Nein,' they say. 'No one leaves Russia anymore.' "

"But why?" Mother wanted to know.

"They do not say. But it is understood . . . they must save face with other countries. 'If Communism is so good, why do so many people want to leave?' "

"What will we do? We should. . . ."

Father raised his hand indicating she should wait for him to finish. "I stopped in Omsk. No passports there, either. But for a 'favor' (a ruble bribe) one man whispered, 'Sneak! Go to Blagoveshchensk . . . cross the Amur River to China. And be quick. There is no time to waste. The GPU (secret police) are arresting all *kulaks*.' "

Speculation gone, now the anticipated exodus became a reality. But, leave Grandfather and Grandmother? And all the relatives? Suddenly I didn't like the idea.

When I heard Father relate what was happening in Moscow, however, I began to look at our escape in a different light. He spoke of endless lines of people waiting to see the Kommisariat of Interior (Minister of Interior); of make-shift huts and unbelievably crowded apartments that failed to accommodate the great number of Mennonites who had sold everything they owned, coming to Moscow in hopes of securing passage to Canada; of meager food rations, of pregnant women who were treated worse than animals.

"Some people are very foolish," Father said. "They go in a big group to the train depot to meet friends and relatives when they arrive. Such laughing and crying when they are united! This attracts the GPU. Come midnight, in black limousine, the police whisk heads of family off to...." He shuddered. "Who knows?

"But I can tell you one funny experience," he continued. "One man's wife was a good friend of a lady interrogator who liked her because she spoke such good Russian. The lady said, 'Tell your husband to take his rejection letter and hide it in a mop. Then when it is morning he should go to the Kommisariat of Interior. Be sure he joins the regular workers when they go into the building. Tell him to push his way through the long lines of people who are waiting and go to ninth floor to the seventh office room.'

"He did ... and the man in charge was so surprised he gave him passports for his whole family.

"But others are not so fortunate. Many families are packed into boxcars and sent home. But why am I talking? We waste time. There is much to do."

There was much for our family and Liese, her husband and two children, to do. Mattresses had to be filled with newly carded wool for the long Trans Siberian railroad trip to Blagoveshchensk. An enormous amount of zweibach must be baked and toasted and tea packed for meals enroute. Father had told us the trains provided hot water so the passengers could make their own tea.

In the midst of this activity Mother became seriously ill. "She can't be sick now," we groaned in despair! Relatives prayed for her recovery. Father paced the floor impatiently. Finally he made what seemed to me an unforgivable suggestion. He told us to ask God to help her get well quickly, or if she wasn't meant to recover, not to allow her to linger very long.

Never, I thought. Not that prayer. How could he be so callous? Should I be guilty of asking that Mother hurry and die?

Six

Destination: Blagoveshchensk

I was relieved and glad when Mother's health began to improve. Father's uneasiness didn't abate, however. I found this difficult to understand. Having been told we would not be able to cross the Amur River until it had frozen enough to make passage safe, I thought the delay of a few weeks during the summer ought not matter so greatly.

"Soon Mama will be well," I told Father one day. "Why should we hurry?"

Father looked at me and shook his head. "You are a foolish girl, Louise," he answered, near anger in his voice. "Can't you comprehend? Henry is an alien. I am an alien. Soon John will become an alien. If the CPU decides to arrest us, *kaput*, it is over for all of us."

Finally, the waiting time was over. Well enough to travel, Mother supervised the last minute packing of food, bedding, mattresses and clothing. The revolver? With us? Just in case.... I saw fear in Mother's eyes.

"Give it to me," Father said. "I will be responsible."

I had known that Father owned the gun, though he kept it well hidden from us children and from the searching eyes of Russian soldiers. But one day when I was making Mother's bed, I ran my hand under the mattress. I felt metal. I jumped back. It was the gun. Then it disappeared. Father must have hidden it someplace where no one could find it.

After I discovered Father owned a gun I asked, "Should Mennonites have guns?" Mother was unhappy that I had learned about it. "Your papa bought it for his protection in the days when he sold big shipments of grain and returned with the many rubles he was paid." And now we were taking the gun with us. Would Father use it if he felt he had to? I shuddered at the thought.

The last item to be packed (carefully, oh, so carefully) was a family heirloom clock. Someone had told Father that he could use it in exchange for a cow when we arrived in Canada.

Then Father called us together for a final warning: "Remember, all of you, should people ask where we are going we will say—to farm country in the East." We had heard about the area to which he referred. There, south and east of the Amur River in the soil-rich land between the Zeya and Bureya Rivers, a group of Mennonite farmers, yielding to free-land and travel-expense enticements, had emigrated following the Bolshevist Revolution. Apparently they believed Communism would not wrap its vicious tenacles around them so far from home base.

We knew that Father meant what he said. We would move to the area if we *had to*. On the other hand we would make every effort to escape to China. Father had heard that a young man, John Bergmann, could guide us across the Amur River. Treacherous, it alternately thawed and froze in winter, building up huge hummocks of ice that would have to be circumvented by horse-drawn sleds during our escape attempt. John Bergmann was experienced in this. He and his brother, Henry, had made several trips across the river.

They had moved to Slavgorod, 350 miles southeast of Omsk, after a hasty sale of property when things grew difficult in the Ukraine. Good business men, having previously operated a cheese factory, they invested their share of the family estate in a mill which extracted oil from various kinds of seeds, particularly the sunflower.

When the First Five-Year Plan was introduced, the government moved to take over private industry as well as private farms. In attempting to secure control of the *Bergmann and Company* mill, officials refused to sign any kind of an agreement with them. Boldly they continued to operate the mill. But when the processed oil was ready for market the men were unable to secure railroad shipping privileges because of government intervention.

They managed to market the oil on their own, however, only to find that without official permission they could not touch the money they had banked when they were paid for the oil.

John and his brother decided to emigrate. But they, like us, were refused passports repeatedly. When their property was confiscated by the Russians, they began black-market treks to the Orient.

Traveling over ice in winter, they brought back razors, silk clothing, pocket watches, photo film and silk hose which they had procured on the black market from merchants in Sachaljan. They sold this contraband merchandise in Omsk. In time a Jewish merchant in Sachaljan found it "profitable" to report the Bergmanns. John was arrested on a train to Omsk. All of his money (except 10 rubles which he had hidden in his cap) and his merchandise were taken from him. He was given a 50-day jail sentence which he reduced by labor—one day of labor for each three days in jail. Since he was a smuggler, he got off with a light sentence. Had he been an escapee, he would either have been sent to a northern Siberian concentration camp or shot.

When he was released, John knew his and Henry's black market days were over. A second offense wouldn't be taken lightly. When John learned that a bachelor friend wanted to escape to China and America he decided he would become a guide. "I will make money so that I, too, can escape to America." he told himself.

Father first learned about John Bergmann at a cooperative union agriculture meeting. Knowing the discretion of John's brother, Gerhard, chief accountant for the organization, Father told him we were going to try to escape. Perhaps John could help us.

"John is a smart man," Gerhard told Father. "After he was released from jail he made a trial run over the Amur to talk to Chinese friends. 'Will you give me papers so I can stay?' " he asked.

" 'We will give you papers,' the Chinese answered.

" 'For my friends?'

" 'For your friends.' "

According to Gerhard, John then helped his bachelor friend escape. Now he was prepared to help others escape also.

"John is the right man to help you," Gerhard assured Father.

I can't adequately describe the emotional trauma we experienced in our secret departure from Ljubimovka. We had to say goodbye to relatives—to Tante Agnes and her children; to Uncle John who said he would never leave the village as he did not anticipate that life would be too difficult under Communist control. We had to say goodbye, too, to Tante Suse, his wife, and cousin Peter; to Grandfather (in poor health) and Grandmother, both of whom must have realized they would never see us again.

I like to believe I had a very special place in Grandfather's heart. Not as great a place as cousin Peter who was named after him, but special nevertheless. I recall that his eyes filled with tears when he put his arm around my shoulder and drew me close. "You are going to be like your mother some day," he told me. I knew why. I resembled Mother who, with her black hair and dark brown eyes, looked like him. "I will miss you, my chatterbox." I flung myself into his arms and wept.

The memory of Grandfather's parting prayer remains forever etched in my mind. "Dear Heavenly Father. Be with my family as they leave on their dangerous journey. Protect them. Send your guardian angels ahead of them to make their way safe."

Then he prayed as much at us children as for us. He pleaded with us to accept Christ as Lord of our lives. I wanted to. Oh, how I wanted to. Yet I hedged. Perhaps it would be easier when we reached China. . . . I will accept Christ then, I promised myself.

Farewells were doubly difficult for the older boys who also had to say goodbye to the girls they had hoped to marry. Torn between leaving or staying, they knew they had no choice but to flee.

I recall the quick, emotion-filled hugs and kisses when the train stopped briefly thirty miles from our home, enabling the boys to say goodbye. The girls wept bitterly as our train sped away from them.

Fighting tears, we turned our attention to arranging the bedding and clothing on the ledge above the train benches that would serve as seats during the day, as beds during the night. We went about this task solemnly, our minds full of questions about the future.

I recall little about the eleven-day/eleven-night train trip. I am sure I passed much of the time telling stories to my niece and nephew, Leisel and Hans. I'm confident, too, that the older boys escaped to some distant car to play their favorite game of cards. And we ate—tea and zwieback at regular intervals. Later, Mother and I agreed, "Once we are in Canada, we'll never drink another cup of tea."

Father who loved to talk to strangers, struck up conversations with other passengers, always guardedly, he told us.

One day he met three men from the sheep country approximately two hundred miles east of Ljubimovka, the village we had left. From their conversation Father learned they had not been affected by the Revolution to the extent we had. Collective farming was not being forced upon them. Nor was private industry threatened.

"They are good men," Father told Mother. "They are White Russians and they have a plan for us to make a living in Blagoveshchensk while we wait for winter."

Mother gasped. So did I. "You tell them we are going to Blagoveshchensk?" she asked, horrified.

Father placed a reassuring hand on her shoulder. "Am I not a good judge of character? I trust these men."

Mother shook her head warily. "It is best you are careful."

"You should trust me," Father answered.

A few days later we learned some of the details of the contemplated plan. These men furnished the wool for sheepskin-lined, Cossack-styled coats manufactured in Omsk. They believed there would be a good market for them in Blagoveshchensk. There, Father could open a retail store in a rented building under Liese's husband's name, *Toews*. It would be too dangerous to use the name *Friesen*.

Though we usually trusted Father's judgment, we had qualms about these plans. Father would have to make a trip to supervise the shipment of the sheepskin-lined coats to Blagoveshchensk. How would he escape detection?

In the days that followed, Father and his new friends spent a great deal of time discussing and finalizing arrangements that would provide sustenance and an alibi for our living in Blagoveshchensk while we waited to cross the Amur River.

One day as we sat speculating about the relatively short distance we still had to travel, the train ground to a screeching halt. We jumped to our feet, eager to learn what had happened.

"Out! Out!" the trainmen shouted. "Take all of your belongings. Tracks ahead are washed away!"

Exceptionally heavy rains had caused the Amur River and its tributaries to overflow their banks and flood a vast area of land over which we still had to travel. We would proceed by steamboat.

The children clapped their hands. "A boat ride, yet!"

What sounded like a lark turned into a nightmare, however. For one thing, we were as crowded in the boat as matches in a matchbox. The boat inched its way through muddy flood waters. Little by little the turbulence took hold. The river became a churning swirling tyrant that grabbed at our boat as if intent on upsetting it. It uprooted trees, lifted buildings from their foundations and hurled them downstream. I saw a barn crumble and vanish. Then a terror-stricken mongrel, clinging frantically to a weather-beaten log, swept past us. Perched on rooftops children separated from their parents and parents separated from their children cried, "Please, please, save us!" We could do nothing. The pilot insisted our boat would capsize if we took another person on board.

Fear churned within me as I watched the top of a huge house sweep toward us. If it struck our boat ...! I held my breath and hid my face in my hands as it plunged close. I felt a jerk. The pilot had swerved just in time.

We reached our destination late that afternoon.

After about an hour's search Father returned to the board landing to tell us he had rented a hotel room in which we could live until we found an apartment. One room for so many people?

"Could you not find a bigger place?" Mother asked.

"Flood refugees are everywhere. We are lucky to find a room." Father answered.

And what a room! Mother shook her head when she saw it. No one needed to tell her it was vermin infested.

She hated lice and bedbugs as much as she hated the devil. I recall how she used to scour the kitchen after a stranger or soldier had taken leave after having been bedded down on straw for the night. "Quick, burn the straw . . . take blankets outside . . . shake good."

Children of Russian farm laborers had attended my first father's school. Mother soon learned that our clothing, particularly underwear, and our hair had to be searched every night in case a stray louse had decided to change living quarters.

"I almost fainted the first time I found a louse in your papa's hair," she told me. "He used to tease me about it. He'd say, 'I scratch my head when I am thinking and you come running with a fine-tooth comb.' "

I nodded. It seemed that fine-tooth combs served as warrants that permitted her to search her children's heads, too.

Somehow we managed to survive the hotel room. I doubt Mother slept much during that interim, however. Someone had to stay awake to pounce on the bigger, bloodier creatures that made their attack in the night.

Seven
Haven of Hope

The apartment into which we finally moved was located in a private compound which had been renovated to help accommodate the many flood victims who needed homes. It belonged to a medical doctor who left the management of the place to his Jewish wife and her mother.

Though it was a vast improvement over the hotel room, its bedrooms were small. Again Mother, Father and Abe, our crippled brother, slept on cots —like those we see in antique shops today, raised at one end like a ski slope—which they had purchased when we arrived. The rest of us bedded down on wall-to-wall mattresses.

"Speak Dutch and German only when we are

71

alone our parents warned us, "Speak Russian to other people."

Again, "If anyone asks why we are here, tell them we can't farm until the flood waters recede." Later it was, "until winter is over."

Before long Father secured rental space and, after a secret trip to sheep country, opened the *Toews and Company* clothing store which provided a livelihood for us while we waited for winter to arrive (and the Amur River to freeze!) The older boys worked in the store during the day. They spent many evenings in a local theater, much to our parents' distress.

Mother kept busy with household tasks, cooking, baking, washing clothes.... We girls helped as much as we could. At least we scrubbed the floors every day. "They should always be clean," she told us.

As often as possible, in spite of don't-go-near-the-water admonitions, George, Nick and I made our way to the Amur River a short distance from our apartment. Directly across the river lay Sachaljan, a Chinese town where we often watched residents dip water along the shore. It was in this city we planned to secure papers granting temporary residence that would enable us to travel in China on our way to Canada. Though Sachaljan was only a mile away, we knew that crossing the river at this point would be suicide. We depended on John Bergmann to find the least dangerous escape route.

In associations with the customers at the store

Father learned how the Russians discouraged escape attempts. Though they preferred arresting an escapee there were times when someone resisted arrest and was shot. When this happened the body was brought to Blagoveshchensk. The next day the victim's name was posted on a prominent bulletin board to warn others how "foolish" it was to try to escape.

On Sundays we worshipped in a Russian Baptist Church where we were warmly received and felt much at home. The pastor preached Bible truths without interference. We were surprised that religious restrictions were not being enforced as they had been in our home village.

We never felt completely at ease in our apartment, however. For one thing our landlady's mother appeared much too concerned about our affairs. Often when we stepped out of our apartment we caught her eavesdropping though she pretended she didn't understand either German or Dutch.

Mother felt kinder to her after her daughter, the doctor's wife, had pointed to the philactery that hung beside the entrance to their apartment and said, "I, too, love God."

As winter settled upon us, the river froze, thawed and froze again.

"When do we go?" we asked, eager to be on our way.

"When we are sure the river will hold us," Father answered. "I am making arrangements."

First he told the boys to find John Bergmann,

who by this time had guided several groups to safety. He didn't know that at that moment John Bergmann was looking for us.

"It was a miracle," Bergmann told us when contact had finally been made. "In a city of 30,000 people, no address, nothing. That night a friend and I decided to go to a movie. While we waited for the theater to open I spied three young men in line ahead of us. They were smoking and joking with each other in German. I nudged my friend who also smoked, (though I do not smoke). 'Those must be the Friesen boys and their cousin, Loewen. Ask them for a light.'

"By the time I had persuaded him to follow my suggestion, the boys had gone into the theater. But we caught them afterwards and learned that they were supposed to be looking for me."

Secretly Father arranged to purchase the four horses and four sleds needed for our escape and to secure bills of sale for them as John Bergmann had instructed. He also had them shod with special shoes in case the ice should prove unusually slippery. Then, when Father gave the word, a distant relative whom I remember only by his last name, Siemens, would arrive with a wagon load of hay to exchange for our no-longer-needed household goods.

Like a caravan, our family would follow the farmer in our sleds. We would act as if we were accompanying him to the area where he farmed. Then, when it was safe to do so, we would break away and make our escape across the river ice.

One night when the boys returned from one of

their theater visits they said, "A Mennonite, named Langeman, saw us on the street. He came up and asked if we were the Friesen boys. When we said yes, he asked where he could find John Bergmann."

"So," Father answered. "Others also want to escape."

Those others included Uncle John, Tante Suse and cousin Peter, who arrived in Blagoveshchensk shortly after this episode, despite Uncle John's previous insistence that he would never leave Ljubimovka. He told us government officials had come to our home to arrest Father *the day after* our departure. But that wasn't the only reason why he decided to leave.

"As the *schulze* (the village magistrate) I attended our council meeting one night," he began. "There the Communist leader told us we must pay still more grain tax. You remember Wilhems?" Father nodded. "He grew very angry. 'That I will never do,' he told the man.

Infuriated, the Communist pointed his finger at Wilhems and said, 'For that you will pay twice the new assessment.' Then he turned to me. 'Mr. Funk, you are instructed to collect twice everyone's assessment.'

"Can you imagine? I should go to relatives and friends and tell them they must pay twice their assessment when they had already given more than they could spare. That I could not do. So, I decided that quick," he snapped his fingers, "that we should go with you to Canada."

One evening, shortly after Uncle John's arrival, we sat chatting about contemplated plans for escape. Mother who stood by the window, suddenly gasped. "Schushe!" she hissed. After a few breathless minutes of suspense she added, "I saw a man with pencil and pad of paper in his hand. Now he is gone. So quick he sneaked away."

The snowy footprints that lead to a nearby apartment were mute proof that someone had been listening to and possibly recording our conversation. "He must be the man I bumped into the other night on my way to the outhouse," Henry said.

The next morning Anna saw the man. He stood across the street obviously intent on watching our every move. Later we learned he had vacated his apartment. A spy? What else?

Our suspicious were verified a few days later when three letters, addressed to *Henry Friesen, John Friesen* and *Henry Loewen* (our cousin) arrived in the mail. Each contained a questionnaire: Why are so many people living in one apartment? How do you make a living? Why aren't you serving in the army? What is your income? Do you have plans to move?

Army induction papers were included in the letters addressed to John and cousin Henry. Why only two? Because Henry had already served time in the army. His questionnaire would verify his identity as *the* Henry Friesen who had been sent home as an alien.

"The boys must flee," Father said. "They cannot wait for us." He promised the boys he would mail the questionnaires when we were ready to leave. This was possible since they had been given thirty days to report to the army.

Before they left Father gathered his family around him and asked us to kneel and pray for the boys' safety. He begged them again to consider giving their lives to Jesus Christ. "We are too young," they answered. "Someday...."

By the time we rose from our knees our faces, even the boys' were wet from weeping. It was like a funeral. We knew we might never see each other again.

"Now wash your tears. No one must know you have been crying," Father told the boys as he handed them money for boat passasge to Canada in case it proved possible for them to proceed without delay.

"Margaretha," I heard him tell Mother after they had left, "I will talk to the partner who promised to continue business as usual when we leave. Then I will send word to Siemens that he should come and pick up things we no longer need. We will go as soon as possible when Bergmann returns."

Not since the day Mother took ill shortly before we left Ljubimovka had I seen Father as tense and worried as he was in the next couple of days. That evening he paced back and forth in the apartment calling on God to be merciful to his children. As unobtrusively as possible, the next morning he left the house to pace back and forth along the river bank. Suddenly to his horror, a border patrolman came riding across the frozen river with the body of a dead man. Toward evening Father checked to see whose name had been posted on the bulletin board.

He returned speedily. "Praise God! Praise God!" he exclaimed. "It was not one of the boys."

A few nights later we were awakened by a stealthy knock on our door. Father pulled on his trousers and went to answer it. "Who?" he whispered.

"John . . . John Bergmann."

"In a minute," Father answered. "Margaretha, get dressed . . . no, you children stay where you are."

While Mother prepared tea for Mr. Bergmann we sat bug-eyed on our mattresses as he told us of the boys' escape! This was his story:

You know we left late in the afternoon of market day so we could mingle with the farmers as they moved out of the city and traveled over the Zeya River back to their farms. Well, something must have happened. No farmers came to the city that day, so none left. We had to set out by ourselves. I wished then the boys had not dressed so well. They should have dressed like farmers as you see I do.

I walked with John in front. Henry and Loewen walked in back. I warned, "If anyone approaches us let me do the talking. I know all about the country south of here."

We were almost across the river when a guard

rode toward us. He passed, then, in an instant, swung his horse around and shouted, "Stop!"

We turned to face him. That put me at a disadvantage. Now I was behind the boys. I stepped forward when the man asked, "What are you loitering here for?"

I acted brave and introduced the boys by their first name only. "We are not loitering. We are going across the Zeya River because this is where the road is. How else can we go? I am supposed to show my friends the farmland in the area where I live. They have a letter from their father telling them to find a good place to farm.

"Where are you going?" the man asked.

"To Konstantinovka."

"And what is Konstantinovka?"

"Are you an officer and do not know Konstaninovka is a big city?" I challenged. The boys stood still. Their faces didn't change color. They hid their nervousness well.

For some reason, I don't know why, the patrolman gave his horse the spur, whirled around and rode off. Perhaps he thought we had weapons. Then we would have had the advantage over him. Or maybe he realized he didn't have any evidence against us. Had he encountered us on the Amur River, it would have been a different story.

I turned to the boys. "Now we must move fast, only do not run."

In the village on the other side of the Zeya River I asked Henry and Loewen to drop back so no one would know we traveled together. Right then, I decided it wasn't safe to continue on our way. It would be better to take advantage of the Cossack village hospitality and ask for lodging for the night in one of the homes. I knew the inn would be too dangerous. For a fee, the lady proprietor there reports suspects to the soldiers.

We walked past many small houses until we came to one with many rooms. We walked through the tall fence gate. "You stay here," I told the boys. "I will go up the steps." All of the village houses have high foundations and many steps to protect them from floods, just like the houses along the Amur and Zeya Rivers in Blagoveshchensk. I knocked on the door. A lady opened it. I told her we wanted a place to stay for the night.

"Wait here," she said. "I am only a visitor. I will take you to my home, but first I must tell my friends goodbye."

She stepped into the house. At that instant a guard on horseback raced down the street looking this way and that. The boys were lucky the fence hid them. Me? I was frightened. But apparently the rider was hunting for four men, not one waiting outside of an open door.

The woman led us to her home. And just like the other time, as soon as we closed her fence gate another guard rode by. The boys thought it was a good joke. They didn't realize how narrowly we had escaped death.

The lady made tea and gave it to us with some

bread. Then she brought straw bedding and blankets. Not accustomed to so much walking the boys were very tired and went right to sleep.

I sat in a chair thinking about our narrow escape when a knock sounded on the lady's door. My hair stood up like a cat's when it meets danger. She opened the door only a sliver. "Oh, it's you cousin Petra," she said. "I am sorry, but I am getting ready to go to bed. You can come back in the morning."

The woman did not listen. She pushed her way into the room. I sucked in a big breath of air. I knew her! She was the proprietor of the village inn, obviously under the influence of liquor.

"Nonsense," she said. "You have time to talk." Then she spied me. "Why are you here?"

I told her what I had told the guard we met on the Zeya River road.

"You talk foolish," she said. "I know where you plan to go."

"Quiet," the lady of the house interrupted. "It is you who talk foolish. I will get some vodka."

She brought liquor, poured a smidgeon in her glass but filled her cousin's to the brim. After several refills the proprietor of the inn staggered home.

I went to bed but not to sleep. Anything can happen, I told myself.

Early the next morning, just before dawn, the lady served us tea and bread again. At the door she winked at me. "Don't worry about Petra. So drunk, she will sleep a long time this morning."

We had walked about a mile south along the

Amur River when we saw a man who, in the dim light, looked like a soldier. "Run to the river," I shouted to the boys. We sped down the bank and onto the ice. When we looked back we saw the man was a farmer carrying a whip behind his back so the tip stuck over his cap like the decoration on a soldier's cap. We kept going at a good speed, around hummocks of ice, across a river island and then over the rest of the ice.

We weren't safe yet, however. When we came to Sachaljan we went to the hotel owned by a Chinese friend. He must have seen us coming for he rushed to the door to stop us from entering "Look through the peephole," he told me. I looked, and there sat the merchants I had bought black market goods from. With them sat a Russian official. We left immediately and didn't come back until the men had gone.

But now your boys are safe on their way to Harbin. By the time you arrive they will be traveling to Canada."

When Bergmann finished his story Father whispered something in his ear. Bergmann nodded. "I will be ready," he said.

Eight
Flight to Freedom

December 1928, D-day morning! Temperature: ten degrees below zero! We bundled up in heavy coats, woolen caps, mittens and above-the-knee felt boots.

Mr. Siemens arrived with a wagonload of hay which he transferred to our box-like sleds in exchange for the household furnishings we had accumulated during our four-month stay in Blagoveshchensk. We spread the hay on the bottom of our sleds to make travel more comfortable and to provide food for the horses. Empty pails (more than we needed to water the horses) were tied to the sides of the sleds to make it appear we were indeed traveling to farm country. Money hoarded from our

Alexanderkron sale and the store enterprise was hidden in Father's and Mother's clothing. "It must be kept intact for passage to Canada," Father explained.

We took a minimum of clothing with us (two willow baskets full), food for the children and the German heirloom clock. John Bergmann, who knew travel hazards from experience said, "Take nothing you can do without."

But the clock *must* go with us. We would need it in Canada. "We will make room," Father told Bergman.

"No, no, not the doll," Liese told her three-year old daughter.

"Yes!" Liesel cried, tossing her long braids and hugging the doll tightly. A small girl shouldn't have to give up her doll, I thought. But, according to our guide it might distract her. She would need to be alert and hang onto the sides of the sled when the going became difficult.

"In Canada I will buy you a new doll . . . a doll with real hair," Liese told her daughter.

Reluctantly the child relinquished her hold on the doll. Mother knelt beside Liesel. "So little to have so much expected of her," she said to herself as she comforted the child.

But Bergmann wasn't through. "Remember you must let me do the talking should anyone stop us." I chuckled—he sounded like Father. "And men, check to make sure you have your horse and sled bills of sale. You, Siemens, go first. We will overtake you on the country road.''

We had prayed and were ready to leave when our landlady called my parents aside. ''You think I do not know where you are going. But I know.''

Mother gasped, fear in her eyes.

''Wait,'' our landlady said. ''You must not worry. I, too, will come there soon.''

John Bergmann and Abe were assigned to the first sled; Uncle John, Aunt Suse and Peter, to the second; Henry Toews, Liese and their two children to the third. Father and Mother and Nellie to the last. The rest of us trudged behind. We would ride only when we tired. When we crossed the Amur River, however, only Abe, Aunt Suse, Liese and her two children, Nellie and Mother (if she was tired) would be permitted on the sleds. It would be too difficult for the horses to pull heavy loads around and over the hummocked ice.

On the road that crossed the Zeya River we met a guard on horseback. Mr. Bergmann fanned the air with his hand warning us to remain calm. Apparently the man believed we were a group of farmers moving to the country, for he did not stop.

Bergmann had suggested we by-pass the Cossack village where the boys had narrowly escaped capture, driving around it close to shore on the Amur River. But, the moment we turned in that direction he shouted in Dutch, ''Quick left!''

Once back on the main road Abe passed the word that he had seen a guard hiding in the bushes, his machine gun leveled at us.

Warily we followed our guide past the lookout tower praying that whoever watched would believe we had merely mistaken our way. I shuddered, realizing death was only a trigger away. We proceeded through the village. Then we stopped to water the horses and feed the children.

This time it was Uncle John who alerted us to danger. "Don't look around," he told us. "Act natural. Speeding toward us is a patrolman. He could be the man who watched from the bushes."

"Pretend we are fixing the harnesses," Father commanded.

The men took his advice and busied themselves as he directed. The patrolman bore down on us. Any minute now ... I closed my eyes. This is the end....

To our surprise, and relief, the man rode past us, head high, eyes looking straight ahead.

"God blinded his eyes," Mother exclaimed.

On the country road we caught up with Mr. Siemens. John Bergmann stopped our sled caravan when we had traveled about two miles from the village. "Ahead is a spot where the farmers collect firewood left when flood waters recede," he told us. "This is the only place for miles where the river bank slopes easy and gentle so the horses can make their descent onto the ice without mishap. We will follow Siemens until he signals us to leave the road. Then to lighten the sleds, all drivers will run beside them." He explained that at this point we were three miles from the opposite shore instead of one as we had been in Blagoveshchensk.

Listening to Bergmann I remembered what Father had said previously about those of us who ran behind the sleds. Now he repeated the warning. "Each is responsible for himself. Should you fall we cannot stop and help you." I've often wondered if he really would have gone on without us. Regardless, his threat inspired caution.

We had traveled just a short distance when our farmer friend stepped down from his wagon perch, raised his right hand three times (the pre-arranged signal to indicate the coast was clear). "Go fast and God be with you!" he called.

We plunged down the embankment.

Easy? Gentle? What then is a steep descent? I thought. Now... across shoreline gravel, sled runners squealing... onto ice as clear as crystal and slippery as grease. Properly shod for such an eventuality, the horses grabbed the ice and shot ahead. John Bergmann wasn't as fortunate. Clutching his horse's reins he began to scoot across the ice like one of today's water skiers. "Hang on! Hang on!" Abe shouted, fright in his voice. I scarcely noticed. I was having enough trouble keeping my own balance.

Reprieve! A section of ice covered with snow. Bergmann regained his footing and led us around and over hummocks of jagged ice onto an island we had to cross.

He forced his horse to break through the thick woods. We ducked branches and fought brambles as

87

we plunged after him. The sleds teetered precariously behind their horses. The children began to cry. "If this is Canada, I don't want a new doll," young Liesel shouted.

At one point Bergmann's sled hit a snag. His horse lunged forward, once, twice... and away! The sudden jolt sent the man sprawling. He released his grip on the reins. "Oh, my Lord!" he cried as he clawed his shoulder. Father ran to see what was wrong as George took off after Bergmann's horse.

Wincing, Bergmann muttered, "That fool horse! He pulled my arm out of its socket." He shook his head sadly. "Leave me. It isn't safe to stay here... too high... you will be detected."

"You talk nonsense," Father countered. "We do not know the way. We hired you. You must go with us. Come... up with you!" He grabbed our guide and set him on his feet. To steady himself Bergmann reached for a tree branch, missed it and fell against a nearby tree. In that instant his arm snapped back into place.

"Thank God!"

We plunged on... down the island embankment. There Mother fell! For a moment all I could think of was Father's warning that we would stop and help no one. But, Nick, who ran beside her, quickly scooped her into his arms and hoisted her onto her sled.

Now onto the hummocked ice again... across the last span of river, then up... again runners squealed on shoreline gravel. A flip of the whip. Up! Up!

"Praise God! Praise God!"

Winded, the horses stopped in their tracks, chests heaving like huge bellows. Quick, wipe away the sweat!

I leaned against Father's sled completely spent, perspiring profusely in spite of the below-zero weather.

I heard a click. Turning I saw Father empty his revolver. He raised his hand and flung the gun across the river. The bullets followed. "Come spring," he announced, "they will be lost forever."

We stood quietly for some time, each busy with his own thoughts. We were free . . . really free. . . . No more religious persecution . . . no more grain tax . . . no collective farms. *Thank you, thank you, Jesus!*

Father broke into our musing. "Now we must pray."

We gathered around him as he thanked and praised God for our protection. Then we sang: "Now thank we all our God. . . ."

We had made it! We were in China!

China! The thought triggered the memory of the resolve I had made to receive Christ as my Savior. *I will . . . I will*, I hedged again. *When we get to Canada.*

"We must not loiter," Bergmann, his face grim with pain, admonished. "I will take you to *fanza* (inn) where we will find food and shelter. Tomorrow we will go to Sachaljan to secure residence permits."

I don't know exactly what I expected of the inn. I had read fabulous accounts about "oriental splendor" but here was nothing but a vermin-infested hovel. An open hearth in the center of one end of the room was used to cook meals and to send warm air through a low, enclosed ledge attached to three walls of the room. We both sat and slept on that ledge.

After a meal of tea, bread and hot soup we bedded down for the night. I doubt I've ever been so weary. Warm on one side, freezing cold on the other, we were grateful, nevertheless, for rest. It had been a harrowing day.

During our three days in Sachaljan, nine miles from the inn and directly across the Amur River from Blagoveshchensk, we stayed in a clean, comfortable hotel, the Wolga, if I remember correctly.

Father soon learned why John Bergmann had insisted he secure bills of sale for the horses and the sleds. Since we had no further use for them and had to dispose of them, we were at the mercy of the Chinese buyers.

After the transaction Father related what had happened. "They want to pay little price. But Bergmann reminded them that they had agreed to pay what we paid for them.

" 'You have bills of sale?' they asked, thinking they would trap us.

"I pulled the bills of sale out of my pocket and then without further questions the Chinese paid the exact amount. Gerhard Bergmann was right. His brother is a smart man."

In spite of his discomfort—he suffered a great deal of pain in his damaged shoulder—he arranged to have the hotel manager secure residence permits for each of us at a reasonable price and to arrange for the rental of a bus that would take us to Tsitsihar, some 350 kilometers away. There we would board a train for Harbin.

There was one thing our guide could not do, however. He could not prevent other passengers from crowding onto the bus though it had been rented exclusively for our group.

The day we left Sachaljan the temperature dropped to twenty below.

John Bergmann said, "Don't expect an easy trip." We didn't, yet none of us was prepared for the twisting, jolting ride across the Lower Kingman mountain range. Our stomachs lurched with the bus. We became nauseated.

Since there were no airline "comfort bags" aboard, Peter came up with ingenious substitutes —men's gloves. They were passed from one bus-sick passenger to the next and emptied when the driver found it convenient to stop.

Enroute we spent three nights in inns similar to the one we had slept in previously. Certainly they were vermin infested, according to Mother who stood watch over us during the night.

Bergmann, who had travelled this route during his black-market days, warned us that bandits roamed the area over which we travelled.

"Not long ago they stopped one of the buses," he said. "They forced all the passengers out.

" 'Lie down on the ground,' they ordered. 'If you so much as raise your head we will shoot.'

"One young boy didn't believe them. He raised his head to take a quick look. He was dead before he knew what had happened to him."

We arrived in Tsitsihar on Christmas Eve. After we had purchased our train tickets to Harbin, we enjoyed a hearty meal of Russian food, a welcome change from our travel fare. Then on to Harbin, a distance of 500 kilometers, arriving there Christmas morning.

Father had just commented about how strange it felt to be entering a city where we knew no one except a doctor friend who had settled in Harbin some years before, when he noticed a young man pushing a railway cart. "If I didn't know better," he said, "I would think that was John."

"It is John," I cried. "And over there is Henry."

"Why? What were they doing here? By this time they should be on their way to Canada."

"Canada won't take us. They've closed their doors to immigrants," John told us bitterly. "What can we do? We have to work cheaply like the coolies who can live on rice only."

Henry glared at Father. Then sounding like one of the wandering Israelites described in Exodus, said, "You forced us to leave Russia and our sweethearts! Is this the promised land?"

Our hearts sank. Not go to Canada? Where then could we go?

nine

People Without A Country

Frightened by the thought of living in such a large city—an important international center then, today Harbin is one of the most densely populated cities in China—and discouraged because we couldn't proceed directly to Canada, we began to look for a place to live.

Arriving when we did, in winter, we were able to rent a two-bedroom summer cottage on an island in the Sungari River. Poorly built, it provided scant shelter from the biting cold and scant furnishings, three cots, a small table and a stove. No chairs. At mealtime members of the family who didn't sit on the cots knelt to eat.

But Mother would not permit us to be sad. It was

Christmas, a time when we should rejoice. Somehow our parents managed gifts—a tangerine, some figs and a few walnut meats for each of us. And because it was Christmas we worshipped in a Lutheran church which was celebrating the birth of the Savior. Accustomed to church in a school, later in our home, we were overwhelmed by the beauty of the sanctuary, by the glittering lights and festive decorations and by the unexpected gifts we received, picture plaques of the Good Shepherd.

Shortly afterward I decided to do some window shopping in Harbin, a new experience for me. When I stopped to look at a display of women's clothing, I felt someone touch my elbow. I turned. Beside me stood a flashily dressed middle-aged man.

"How do you do?" he said, using the Russian language. "Would you like me to buy you a drink?"

"I do not drink." I answered and hurried away.

Later when I stopped to examine a theater display I discovered him at my side again.

"Shall we go in and see the picture?"

"Oh, no!" I exclaimed dismayed that I had even stopped to read the advertisement. He grabbed my arm. "If you come with me I will buy you some nice new clothes. You are a very attractive young woman."

I turned and ran. The implication of his suggestion seared my soul. *Attractive?* Humph! Not according to my family. If I hadn't been so frightened I might have laughed. I never again window-shopped alone.

"Now we must look for a country that will agree to take us," Father told us one day. He tried to sound optimistic but I am sure he was as worried as we that we might have to stay in Harbin forever. "But first, all of us who can must look for work. We cannot use the funds we will need for our boat passage."

Many people, some White Russians and a few Mennonites had managed to leave Russia and emigrate to Harbin prior to the Russian Civil War. One of the Mennonites, Dr. John Isaac, an opthalmologist and a personal friend of Father's, took us under his wing and offered to help us any way he could.

He informed us that, since many of the Russians were prosperous, their wives and the wives of wealthy Chinese often hired girls to care for their children and to help with the housework.

Unskilled at anything but housework, I began to look for such work—rather eagerly I must admit. Mennonite women in Ljubimovka and Alexanderkron occasionally hired Russian girls to work for them. Treated well and given food, clothing and a small salary, they had always seemed contented in their work. Now, even though my salary would be used for family expenses, I, too, would be able to work away from home.

How naive can one be? I soon learned that wealthy Russian and Chinese women in Harbin differed greatly from Mennonite women in their treatment of working girls. Pay was low, fifteen yen a day; the work back-breaking. I scrubbed floors, did the laundry (by hand) and cared for the children who often treated me worse than a dog. Some nights I became so homesick for our old life I wished we could retrace our steps and return to Russia. I was beginning to feel like the older boys. Who cared, if we had only our "leeks and onions" to eat?

To make matters worse, Father's partiality toward Anna flared anew. Someplace he heard that girls who learned silk picture artistry could make good money in other countries.

"I have decided Anna should take lessons," he said.

Excited, I asked if I could take them, too.

He shook his head. "No, we can spare money only for Anna's lessons."

I clenched my fists. My resentment for my stepfather leaped another notch. For so long I'd heard: "It is God's will that we leave Russia." Was it? I wondered. Wasn't Father responsible for our plight? Blinded by self-pity I chafed in the role in which I was forced to continue.

One day I heard my employer tell a friend she had recently learned that the Chinese girl whom I had replaced had been sold by her father for $100 to a man for.... She stopped. "You know what," she told her friend.

I knew I'd never be sold that way. Yet why should Anna always be favored? I recall how on one of my visits home, I burst into uncontrollable weeping. Mother, who rarely showed her feelings, embraced me.

"Why do you cry, Louise? Tell Mama."

I shouldn't have, but I did. I described my work, my jealousy of Anna and her place in our home.

"Louise, Louise, you think foolish thoughts. Your Papa loves you, too. It is only that Anna is his child. He is afraid we will be unable to leave China. If Anna learns new work, Papa can buy some sewing machines and start a new business.

I took her advice and it was good to be home again no matter for how short a time. It was during this interim that our family became involved in what I considered a major catastrophe. Somehow the older boys had been persuaded they could be as ingeniously successful selling meat processed from sheep as Father had been in selling sheep-skin lined coats in Blagoveshchensk. "Buy cheap from farmers, bring to city and sell for a good price," someone suggested.

The problem: the meat was mutton, not lamb, and as such sold poorly. But, someone had to eat it. Mennonites do not waste food. Fortunately, or perhaps I should say unfortunately, the cold weather preserved the meat. Imagine, mutton seven days a week!

By now news of our safe arrival in Harbin had filtered back to the Slavgorod/Barnaul Colony. Mennonites, alone or as families, began to arrive in the city. Through them we discovered that the Russians were clamping down on all emigration. Public auctions of farm animals, equipment and home furnishings were forbidden. Railroad tickets were difficult, in many places impossible, to obtain.

Mr. Aaron Langeman, who turned up in Blago-veshchensk before we fled, arrived in Harbin shortly after we did. He told how he had tricked the Russians into granting him permission to buy tickets for his family. It was impossible to keep from laughing as he strutted back and forth in our small quarters, looking for all the world like Stalin himself. Head high, broad shoulders thrown back, he related his experience:

I went to our village council meeting one evening hoping and praying our Communist representative had not discovered I had bought my grain tax allot-ment on the black market.

When the chairman of the meeting arrived he walked behind the chair where I was sitting. Stoop-ing as though intent on fastening a boot strap, he whispered the warning signal, "Aaron, your *cup* is *full*."

My heart beat wildly. I could hardly wait for the meeting to end so I could rush home and tell my wife, Agatchen, that now I was a marked man. We must flee.

"How will we get money for boat passage?" she asked when I had explained what had happened.

"I know a man who will auction our furniture, a few pieces at a time, for a commission," I said. Living in a village some distance away he was eager to make money on the side. So each night under cover of darkness I loaded a few of our belongings into a sled and, shaking in my boots every inch of the way, delivered the load to my "benefactor."

After each delivery I collected my share of the money earned in the previous sale. Never really confident we could trust the man, we lived in constant fear that we would be apprehended.

Agatchen was sure we were in trouble the day a Communist official called and asked to see me. Agatchen was beside herself with fear. What would happen if he forced his way into a nearly empty house? As calmly as possible she told him I was not at home and that she did not know when to expect me. He left saying he would call another day.

By this time a wild plan had begun to fill my mind. I reminded Agatchen that the wife of the Chairman of Transportation had spent several summers on her parent's farm because of ill health.

"I will go to Omsk and ask this man for permission to buy tickets to Blagoveshchensk."

She shook her head. "You'll never get to see him. His office is on the third floor of a strongly guarded building."

"I can try," I answered.

Having been attached to both the Red and White armies in hospital detail I knew how Russians defer to authoritative, prestigous people. So, I made prestigious plans of my own. One Saturday I rode my horse to Omsk. I bought high-topped boots, a karakul fur cap and a smart Cassock coat with a karakul collar. Then I slipped on some impressive looking full-length gloves and called a taxi to take me to the transportation building.

Upon arrival I cocked my cap to one side and marched up to the gate entrance. I gave the guard a condescending look and brushed him aside. Flabbergasted, he let me pass. So far so good. At the entrance door, however, I was stopped.

"Your permit?" the guard asked.

I lowered my voice and glared at the man. "You ask *me* for *my* permit? Do you not know who I am?" I challenged brusquely in Russian.

Properly cowed, he let me in. When I reached the third floor I went up to another guard. Authoritatively I asked to be directed to the chairman's office. Also impressed, he showed me to the door.

I knocked.

"Come in," a deep voice ordered.

I'll never forget the expression on the man's face when I strode into the room.

"How did you get in?" he asked.

I shrugged. "I walked in." I'm not positive, but I believe I saw a twinkle in the man's eyes. He told me to be seated.

"What do you want?"

I didn't hesitate. Boldly I told him, "I want five tickets to Blagoveshchensk. The ticket agent will not sell them to me without a permit."

The man made a steeple with his hands and for several minutes sat staring over them at me. I can tell you I was plenty frightened. He could decide either way.

Suddenly, he reached for the phone and placed a call to the railroad station. Thirty minutes later I had the tickets in my pocket.

And so they came, one after the other. A Russian school teacher surprised us when he came to call. He had traveled to Blagoveshchensk to visit with Anna. Learning we had fled he decided to follow us.

In another instance, a family from the farm area east of Blagoveshchensk escaped during a blinding snow storm, believing the snow would provide the protection they needed to successfully cross the Amur River.

The moment they hit the river, however, bullets began coming thick and fast. Voices shouted for them to stop. One of the brothers thought he saw a border guard pursuing them, but he couldn't be certain. Urging their horses to maximum speed they managed to outdistance the gun fire. But when they reached the opposite shore their parents failed to make their appearance. It wasn't until months later that they learned that their father had been arrested and jailed.

When the parents of the girl who later became Nick's wife arrived, we learned that they and their eight children, one a three-month old baby, had left a barn full of livestock and food cooking on the stove to make it appear they had merely stepped off the place for a short period of time. Other refugees, we discovered, had practiced the same kind of trickery.

The Rogalskys—Henry, his pregnant wife, Anna, their three children and another girl they cared for—arrived with a group of 61 men, women and children who had escaped from Slavgorod.

They had waited as long as possible for Anna Rogalsky to give birth to her child. When the baby failed to arrive according to schedule they decided, to proceed as planned, because of previous arrangements and fear that the Amur ice would melt.

Previously Mrs. Rogalsky had prayed, "Please God, let my baby be born before we leave," now she pleaded, "Oh, Heavenly Father, you are all powerful. Please help me to carry my baby as far as Blagoveshchensk."

Because train tickets could only be purchased for short distances in their area, members of the group staggered destination points to avoid suspicion. They repeated this procedure until they arrived in Blagoveshchensk. There they scattered to several rental facilities (again to avoid suspicion) until arrangements could be made to escape. They traveled three days and three nights north and east, bypassing the route we had taken in our flight. By this time it was so heavily guarded that no one dared use it to escape.

At this point Mrs. Rogalsky asked God to let her carry her baby until they arrived in Sachaljan. After that it was "until we get to Harbin." In each inn she repeated the prayer. She couldn't imagine delivering her baby in such filthy hovels—surrounded by 61 travel companions!

On the last stretch of their bus trip, the vehicle in which she was riding broke down. In despair she got out of the bus to stand shivering, hugging her bulky body as if to protect her unborn child from the cold. *I should have stayed in Blagoveshchensk*, she chided herself. *What will I do now*?

A young man on one of the other buses settled the question by offering to change places with her.

"It was a miracle," Anna Rogalsky exclaimed as she shared the news. "By the time the broken bus arrived in Harbin I had given birth to Mary, the baby I had carried close to ten months. No, it wasn't I . . . it was God. He willed it so."

Where were all these people meant to go? No one knew. Though Father had been investigating one lead after another, we learned that other Mennonites were doing the same thing. Three men in particular, Aaron Warkenton, his brother, Isaac, and a man named, Aaron Mickelson, sought help from both the Japanese and the German consulates in Harbin. They were turned away (neither country wanted us) with the suggestion that they try the United States.

Nudged by Dr. Isaac, Father, too, ended up at the U.S. Consulate. The consul suggested the men get together and "choose one of your group capable of expressing himself well enough to present defendable reasons for leaving Russia and adequate reasons why you wish to settle in the United States. Tell this person to write a letter to our consulate at Riga, Latvia." Why Riga? At that time it was the emigration processing center for Eastern Europe.

Most of the Mennonites in Harbin were farmers with little formal education. Who among them could formulate a convincing enough letter to persuade the United States to favorably consider our plight?

Dr. John Isaac believed Father could. If there was any disagreement about this choice, and there may have been, I was not aware of it. In any case, Father got the job.

He immediately sat down and composed a letter in Russian, later translated into English, enumerating the reasons why we had fled Russia and why we wished to emigrate to the United States. He stressed the fact that the majority of our people were frugal, industrious farmers who would be a credit to the nation.

Few people know exactly what happened after that. Apparently Fridtjof Nansen, the famous arctic explorer and humanitarian, became interested in us and in the Armenian refugees (also people without a country) who had fled Turkey. It was he who prevailed on Herbert Hoover, then President of the United States, to help us. Two Mennonites, P. C. Hiebert and M. B. Fast, who had been in Russia during the famine, also pleaded our cause.

In time we were notified that we would be permitted, a few at a time, to emigrate to the United States. However, there were stipulations which we had to fulfill: each person must be able to pay his own way and guarantee that he was physically able to care for himself. No ill or handicapped persons would be given asylum.

Since many of the Mennonites had fled with empty purses, they had no money for boat passage. They were unable to provide food for their families in Harbin. Each day found them in Red Cross food lines grateful for whatever they received.

Because Father had money not only for himself, but for his family, it was decided that he and a brother of Dr. Isaac, James Isaac, should go to the United States and appeal to the Mennonite Brethren for loans for those who would need them. We would follow Father as soon as he sent for us.

By this time Mother, ordinarily patient and long-suffering, had reached a point of despair. Alone, now that Father had left on this mission, she chafed under the confinement of our small quarters where it seemed she waged an endless war against roaches and bedbugs.

One day our landlady, knowing we might soon be leaving, came to inspect our home. A small, bantum-rooster type of woman, she scolded Mother fiercely when she discovered red flecks on the walls. Though Mother rarely lost her temper she did then. She placed her hands on her hips and glared at the woman. "You tell me another way to kill them!" she challenged.

Unable to refrain from laughing at Mother's outburst, I fled the room. No doubt Mother made her peace with the woman. I'm confident, however, that she signed no truce with the bloody nighttime invaders.

But it wasn't only roaches and bedbugs that

troubled her. One day I saw her touch Abe's shoulder, tears in her eyes. Then I understood. The emigration stipulation: only those who are physically able to care for themselves! What, then, would happen to Abe?

Ten
United States,
Here We Come!

Then a letter came from Father, brimming with exciting news. He owned an automobile! We had dreamed of such good fortune, but scarcely dared believe it would ever materialize.

When he arrived in San Francisco he was told an automobile would enable him to make contacts in behalf of Harbin's stranded Mennonites more easily.

"I have a Harbin driver's license," his companion, James Isaac, told him. "Dr. John helped me to get it. I often drove his car."

"And I have enough money," Father answered.

It took very little persuasion on the part of the car salesman to convince him he should purchase a

1928 Chandler. After an around-the-block, mini-driving lesson, the men set off for Reedley, California, where they heard that earlier Mennonite emigrants and their descendants were already well established on farms.

Years before in Russia, Father had read that a retired missionary couple who had served in India, Mr. and Mrs. Frank Wiens, had retired in Reedley. Surely if anyone could help them, they could. The fact that he had heard nothing about them in recent years or that he didn't know on which street they lived didn't faze him.

"Reedley isn't such a big city. I will find them," he told James Isaac.

The men had gone only a short distance when drivers who passed them either honked their horns or shouted at them as they pointed toward their car. Mr. Isaac pulled to a curb and got out to investigate. Smoke! Was the car on fire? Not so, Mr. Isaac had merely forgotten to release the emergency brake.

Totally confused by U.S. highway signs which they did not understand, the men often strayed from Highway 99, their route of travel. However, eventually they reached Reedley, their destination.

Upon entering the city Father suggested they drive to the residential area. As they approached 11th Street, he said, "Stop the car. Wait here. I will go and find out if any Mennonites live in the city." With that he took off down the street.

Father wrote that he knocked on one door after

another asking if by chance the occupants were Mennonites and if they knew where Mr. and Mrs. Frank Wiens lived.

He found Mennonites. He also found Mrs. Wiens, whose husband was now deceased. She lived on 11th Street!

"I'll be right back," Father told her when he explained who he was. Then he turned and ran back to the car. As he approached it he waved excitedly, shouting, "James! The town is full of Mennonites!"

It was, and they helped him. Knowledgeable persons directed him to the Mennonite Brethren Emigration Committee with whom he made arrangements for loans to be extended to persons stranded in Harbin without funds. Because Father had purchased our train and boat tickets before he left we were free to leave as soon as we were able.

United States, here we come!

It all seemed like a wild, impossible dream. As a family we tried to recall all we had heard or read about this country which was to become our permanent home.

I looked at my hands, swollen and sore from wringing the clothes I had laundered in the Chinese home where I worked. Even if Father secured a housekeeping job for me as he said he would, there would be *washing machines*. And all the candy we could eat . . . and fruit, oranges! I had had only one orange in my life and that I had shared with my school teacher. I recall I ate the peelings as well as the pulp. How should I know they weren't considered edible? Now I would enjoy juicy, ripe oranges every day. Surely, we decided, the United States must resemble the land of milk and honey described in the Bible.

None too soon the departure date, August 24, crept upon us. Sorrow cast a shadow over our joy, however. Abe, who had been hospitalized for some weeks, would be unable to accompany us. Not because of his present bout with illness, but because all handicapped persons were denied entrance in the United States at the time. Though our Russian friend had promised to take care of him, parting was something we would have liked to avoid.

We went to the hospital to say goodbye to Abe the day before we were to leave Harbin. When we entered his room we found him playing his mandolin, his most treasured possession. We had been told we must make every effort to remain composed, yet in that moment of parting there were tears in spite of our efforts to control our emotions. I was so overcome with love for this crippled brother I thought I would burst. I ran to him, threw my arms around him and hugged him hard. Then I wept.

"Don't cry, Louise," he said. "Soon I will be well enough to travel. A month or two, then I'll see you again."

He turned to Henry who stood nearby. "Here." He handed him the mandolin. "Take it to America for me. When I come I will have all I can do to manage my crutches."

Henry hesitated. I sensed his thoughts. He ought

to refuse—Abe would need the instrument more than ever after we were gone. But to refuse might prove disastrous. Abe might guess we didn't expect to see him in America very soon, though we prayed the U.S. might relent and permit him to come at some later date.

Henry accepted the mandolin reluctantly. "I'll take good care of it for you, Abe." He turned aside to hide his tears.

When we left, Mother lingered behind. Joining us shortly afterward she literally stumbled out of the room, blinded by tears she could not control. They were tears symbolic of those that would flow every time she thought of Abe and the hopelessness of a situation about which she could do nothing.

The next day we boarded a train that took us through Manchuria and Korea to Pusan, the seaport city on the southeast tip of Korea. From Pusan we traveled by boat to Shiminoseki, then by train to Kobe where, after doing some sightseeing, we spent the night. What a strange city, we thought—cars and bicycles darting through the streets . . . people everywhere . . . picturesque shops and intriguing shrines. . . .

I don't recall having purchased anything, yet I or one of our party must have, for I own a silk fan and a small jewel case reminiscent of our stop in that city.

In the morning we boarded an ocean liner, the *Tenyo Maru* which would take us to San Francisco via Yokohama and Honolulu. What a sight we must have been. Girls and women in long drab dresses; boys with short cropped heads, the style in China. A handful of baggage, an heirloom clock, and hearts full of both hope and apprehension.

We traveled third class close to the motors where it was hot and dreadfully noisy. Depressing, too, with a maze of pipes on the ceiling and walls of our compartments . . . tiered bunks and just-above-sea-level portholes that spat salt water at us when we opened them to get a whiff of fresh air.

Several American young men, a troupe of black entertainers who had just completed a tour of Japan, and a young woman, twenty or twenty-one years of age, traveled with us. For the most part the young men kept to themselves. The young woman, who for some reason had been assigned third class accommodations though she had expected first, either ignored us or treated us with disdain.

We got along famously with the black passengers, however, even though they were a novelty to us and neither they nor we spoke each other's language. They played games with us. When Mother wasn't looking, they taught me how to play cards. One evening they went through their song and dance routine. I shall never forget the experience. I imagine Mother's stern scolding helped etch it in my mind.

We crossed the International Date Line on my fifteenth birthday. With help from our steward who smuggled sweet pastries into our quarters, I celebrated the occasion two days in a row. My kind

benefactor told me that were we crossing the
equator he would see that I was initiated into the
Order of the Golden Dragon.

"And what is that?" I asked.

He described in great detail variations of a tradi-
tional ritual where an officer dressed and throned as
King Neptune orders the shaving and dousing of
innocent travelers.

"Then I am glad we do not cross the equator on
this trip," I told him.

I had looked forward to meals on board ship.
Since they came with our tickets I'd be able to eat
all I pleased. (In Russia I had not only decided I
wouldn't drink tea in America, I had decided I'd
never turn down food.) But I found the Japanese
menu, fish, more fish and rice didn't please me as
it does now. Twice a week we were served European
food, however, and except for members of the family
who succumbed to seasickness, we enjoyed these
meals. I learned how to pronounce the word, *vinegar*,
after I discovered this strange liquid enhanced the
flavor of the cooked cabbage I ate.

Traveling in "steerage" as our quarters were
called, would have been devastatingly boring had it
not been for frequent skirmishes into forbidden first,
second and deck-promenade territory.

"Come, Louise," Nick would call. "Let's get
some fresh air."

"Wait, I'll find George." No use looking for
Nellie. She'd never leave Mother's side. Besides,
we weren't about to let Mother know where we were

going.

On deck I'd throw my head back and let the ocean breeze whip against my face as I raced along the deck with the boys. Once, winded, I sat down in a deck chair to rest, stretching my feet in front of me as other passengers did. Suddenly I felt an insistent tap-tap on my shoulder. A top-heavy woman with a book under her arm peered at me sternly over halfmoon glasses. She made shooing motions with her hands.

I jumped to my feet. Immediately an elderly gentleman, who sat some distance away, rose, crooked his finger and beckoned me to follow him. He led me to an area where there were several long rectangular courts with numbered triangles at each end. There his wife waited for him. They began to play a game which I discovered is called shuffle-board. Their cues sent pucks scooting across the playing area into sections of the numbered triangles. I soon learned that the sum of the numbers scored determined which person won or lost the game. Today, whenever I see anyone play shuffleboard my heart is warmed by the memory of this man's kindness.

We docked in Honolulu for a day. Though many of the passengers, including our older brothers, went ashore to sightsee or shop, Mother kept close tab on those of us who were younger, lest we stray. She did join us on deck, however, to watch the Hawaiian swimmers dive for money thrown by the passengers into the bay.

Once on our way again, we were given a generous

supply of fruit, enough to last until we reached San Francisco. We literally gorged ourselves on it, relishing the bananas and the pineapples most. Their fresh, fascinating flavors were new to us.

After we had eaten our fill, Mother apportioned what remained. Each must have an equal share. George and I consumed ours without delay. Nellie and Nick hoarded theirs—action which proved unfortunate for them. As we neared San Francisco the steward warned us that no fruit could be taken ashore. Since Nellie and Nick weren't able to eat all that they had hoarded, the rest of us gladly assisted them.

Early the morning of September 13, 1929, we were told we were approaching San Francisco, the city of Golden Gate fame. However, we had just begun to get used to the idea when fog enveloped our ship and forced us to lie at anchor for three hours. In that time, I rehearsed what Father had said before he left for America. "Louise, I will find housework for you so you will have a job when you arrive." If American women treated their maids as badly as the Harbin Russians, I thought, I'd rather die than work for them. In sudden panic, I almost wished the ship would sink then and there. But it didn't. The fog lifted and as we scrambled onto the deck we were delighted by what we saw—tall buildings against a background of home-studded hills; boats of all descriptions; seagulls by the thousands. What would this new world be like? we wondered.

Any moment we'd be able to see Father. In spite

of all I've said, I actually looked forward to our reunion. We pulled into Pier #26.

"Look, there's Papa!"

"Don't push. I'm first."

"Hi, Papa!"

He saw us and waved but didn't come near. We soon learned why. First we had to go through customs. Then after our belongings were searched we were taken to Angel Island where we were told we would spend the night. Disappointed, we didn't believe there was anything "angelic" about such a delay.

After our passports were scrutinized we were given a thorough physical examination. Doctors also checked us over to make sure we weren't bringing any lice ashore. I recall that Mother bit her lip during this particular procedure, no doubt stifling a charge which could have been interpreted, "You think we are not clean people? Do you not know we hate lice as much as you do?"

That evening we enjoyed a dinner fit for a king. Yes, we thought, the United States was a *good* place to come to.

To our surprise and *delight*, I'm ashamed to admit, our snobbish travel companion hit a snag. Apparently she was attempting to enter the country illegally with forged credentials of some sort. Consequently she was denied entrance into the United States.

The next morning after urine specimens had been examined we marched between two doctors who checked to see if they could detect any muscular or bone irregularities.

When the boat whistle signalled our departure we discovered Liese's husband, Henry Toews, had been detained. Liese was frantic. She wanted to go back to find out what was wrong. An officer detained her.

At the very last moment Henry came running up the gang plank waving his right arm. "It's that old injury," he told us. "Long ago I fell from a load of hay and broke my arm."

"It was never set properly," Liese amended.

"The doctors noticed it was crooked and made me prove I could use it without difficulty."

Finally we were on our way back to the pier and reunion with Father. And what a reunion! At last we were together again. Now on to Reedley, where preparations had been made to receive us.

Some of the group rode with Father, others were assigned to automobiles driven by friends who had come to take us to our new home. "Here, Nick and Louise, is the man who will take you to the home where you will stay for the night," Father told us.

The man welcomed us warmly in Dutch. "My wife will have dinner ready for us when we arrive," he said.

Dinner did wait us when we arrived. But more important, freedom waited for us—freedom from oppression and freedom to love and worship the One who had so graciously led us to this land of beginning again.

EPILOGUE

A New Beginning

A well known German proverb claims: *Aller anfang ist schwer*—all beginnings are difficult.

This is certainly true when it comes to adapting to the customs of a foreign country. Our trip to Reedley unveiled an entirely new life to us. We exclaimed excitedly about everything we saw.

"Look, farm houses are far apart—not close together as they were in our village in Russia."

"And such strange trees! What are they?"

"Apricots there...." Later, "Peaches... walnuts... almonds."

"And grapes?"

Were my eyes deceiving me? The huge oblong packages which dotted some of the fields... they looked like ... hay! But they couldn't be. I nudged Nick and pointed at one of the fields. "Ask the man what the packages are," I whispered.

Our driver chuckled. "Did you guess they are hay? If you did you are right. Hay, pressed together and tied into bales with wire."

"For what?"

"For easy stacking and storing. Later they will be fed to the cows."

Pretty fancy cows, I thought, suddenly remembering the heirloom clock which, together with some clothing and dishes, was being shipped to Reedley by express. Perhaps we would need more than the clock to get a cow. Then what would we do? Our big family needed large quantities of milk so it was essential that we obtain a cow immediately.

In Reedley we stopped in front of a large white farm home separated from the main road by a row of orange trees. Roses, pink, yellow and crimson, bordered the walk that led to the front door which swung open as we approached it. Our hostess, a short plump woman, smiled broadly as she extended her hand to greet us. "Hello," she said in English.

Nick and I stepped back, appalled. Of what was she accusing us? We had done nothing we needed to be ashamed of.

Apparently she didn't sense our dismay for, speaking Dutch, she smiled again and invited us into the dining room to enjoy the sumptuous dinner of meat, potatoes and gravy she had prepared for us.

"*Hello* must be a good word, not bad like Dutch

halo.'' Nick whispered. I nodded thinking how many times Father had scolded. ''Halo, wo sit it yunt ut?'' (*Now* what have you done?'')

Before we retired, our hostess suggested that we have devotions together. Certainly we wanted to thank God for all he had done for us. We nodded agreement. The woman read a portion of Scripture, then she thanked God for protecting us on our long journey to the United States. When she finished she hesitated as if waiting for us to add our own prayers of thanksgiving. Nick and I remained silent. I knew the only prayer I had a right to pray was wrapped up in the Bible verse: ''Restore unto me the joy of my salvation.''

God had done what I asked him to do, yet I seemed to be unable to keep my promise to him. I found myself wishing the woman would reach over, touch me and ask, ''And why don't you pray?'' I am sure I would have told her I needed to mend my broken relationship with God.

The next day, Sunday, Nick and I were awakened by the woman's cheery voice. ''Breakfast!'' she called.

Breakfast must be the first meal of the day I thought. As soon as I was seated I felt Nick's foot nudging mine, a what-do-we-do-now look in his eyes. On the table in front of us were bowls that contained miniature bales of hay! Cow food! Did the lady expect us to eat it? If so, how? Mother had told us to watch to see what others did before we began to eat. We waited.

Noticing our hesitation our hostess handed me a pitcher of milk. "Pour this on your cereal," she said. "Then sprinkle some sugar on it."

We did as she told us, then waited for her to begin to eat. I broke off a piece of the hay with my spoon as she did. It felt like sharp slivers against my tongue. I took another spoonful. By now the bale had soaked up some of the milk. Each spoonful tasted better than the last. Perhaps cow food wasn't so bad after all.

Later we joined our family for our first United States worship service in the Reedley Mennonite Brethren Church, the church to which many of the residents belonged. We made another discovery. No solemnity here. People waved and shouted greetings as they met outside of the church. Inside the pews were separated by two aisles. The men sat on one side, the women on the other, as we had done in Russia. Apparently the middle section was reserved for the young people. I recall slipping into the very last pew. I bowed my head and prayed. Then I looked around. What kind of a church is this? I asked myself. Everyone so relaxed, some even whispering —in church! A terrible offense to my other-world thinking. I saw a girl my age poke a friend and nod in my direction. I felt my face flush. I sensed we were on display.

Just then the pastor announced the opening hymn. Suddenly, for the first time, I became aware of the lovely organ music, though it must have been playing when we entered the church. When the pastor made the announcements he said, "Today it is our pleasure to welcome the first of a group of Russian refugees who will be coming to our country." I bristled. I wanted to stand up and shout, "We are not Russians, we are Dutch Mennonites."

I could have added (as I did on many occasions in the days that followed), "If a cat has kittens in an oven, that doesn't mean they are cookies!"

After the service, worshippers lingered, visiting together. Wasn't this irreverent? I thought. Didn't they know they should go directly home and ponder the message they had heard?

Our new home belonged to a Mennonite Brethren lay-minister who had offered to employ us on his fruit ranch. Father hadn't needed to find house work for me!

Members of the church had helped furnish our home, donating the necessary dishes, clothing, silverware, pots and pans for our use.

The next morning we went to work harvesting our benefactor's figs. Looking back I realize our work resembed that of migrant workers. When the figs were harvested we moved into the olive orchards, then to the orange groves, picking, sorting, packing as we were instructed. Thus we had employment the year around.

Our pay? A dollar a day per person, $7 for the entire family. Though most people considered this a "depression" wage, we thought of it as manna from heaven. With it Father fed and clothed his large family. Besides he sent fifty dollars a month to

Harbin, China, to pay for Abe's support. "Perhaps," Father suggested, "someday we will be able to purchase a farm of our own."

Just when we felt we were making progress in that direction, Abe wrote asking Father to send him $900. "I have a chance to go to Germany where I am promised I will be cured," he told us. Kind friends who heard of Abe's plight offered to loan us the money he needed.

Despite the hard work, it wasn't long before we began to feel we belonged. Though I enjoyed my new friends, I wasn't entirely happy. My conscience was uneasy. I had a promise to keep and I delayed keeping it . . . until an evangelist visited our church. Unable to resist the Holy Spirit's prodding any longer, I turned my life over to God to use in any way he saw fit.

He saw fit to urge me to ask my brothers to forgive me for provoking them on so many occasions. He saw fit, too, to force me to face up to the dislike, antagonism and self-pity that had plagued my life ever since Mother married my step-father. This doesn't mean that he changed. But I changed. I became more perceptive. What if he hadn't been the determined individual he was? I asked myself. Had he been as gentle and as easy-going as my first father we might never have fled Russia. I shuddered at the thought.

In time, this understanding of Father took on a new dimension—compassion. Accustomed to being the leader, the best farmer in the community, the decision maker, now Father was considered no better than any other farm laborer. He took orders from others, received the same wages as his children. He felt demeaned and I felt sorry for him.

Besides, here was work he knew little about. A grain farmer, he chafed under the new role he was forced to assume, in a climate he felt he would never become accustomed to.

None of us were surprised when he decided to purchase, on loan, a 300 acre alfalfa farm near Patterson, California. Plunging prices forced him to give up this venture, however. Later he achieved a measure of success on an apricot ranch and was able, in time, to clear up our debts and to trade our old Chandler for a new Chevrolet.

I recall sitting on the front porch of our Patterson home, face lifted toward the moonlit sky, crying until I could cry no more. I felt hedged in, squeezed into a characterless mold. And I wanted to be *me*.

"Where are you God?" I asked again. "Speak to me. Show me what you want me to be."

I sensed that he had a plan for my life. Yet I found it extremely difficult to wait for him to reveal that plan. I suppose I didn't understand that I had a great deal of growing up to do before I was ready to serve him as I should.

Some of that growing occurred in the Patterson Evangelical Covenant Church (Swedish Covenant at that time).

"Here is where we shall worship," Father decided.

"But what about the Sundays when services are in the Swedish language?" we asked.

"It will not matter. Their Bible is the same as ours. Besides they are good, kind people in that church." Apparently other people felt as Father did. I recall meetings where worshippers prayed in Danish, German, Dutch, and Swedish.

All Russian escapees were not as fortunate as we. Pressured to safeguard American jobs for American workers during those depression days, the government suddenly halted emigration after only 250 Mennonites had been allowed to enter the United States. This left close to 1000 Catholic, Lutheran, and Mennonite refugees stranded in Harbin.

Later, with Paraguay's consent, a large group of Mennonites, many of them relatives of persons who came to America, moved to this South American country. There they built a new life for themselves under circumstances as trying as our early American settlers.

In 1933 we learned that Abe's trek to Germany for medical care had been fruitless. He passed away shortly before his brother, John, who succumbed to an advanced case of tuberculosis neither he nor we suspected he had. Father died shortly afterward.

"Such a strong man," George told friends the day of the funeral. "I am glad he was my father."

After Father's death we moved to Dinuba, California, a town next door to Reedley, so we could be near our relatives.

It was there I fell in love with a Mennonite boy,

kind, gentle Herbert Nickel.

I was delighted when he taught me how to drive a car. Soon afterwards we decided to visit our relatives and announce our engagement.

"You drive," he urged.

Because it has been raining the road was slick and the shoulders soft. As we approached the rear of a car traveling in the same direction as we, I asked, "Shall I pass?"

"Of course."

I honked the horn and proceeded to pass. In that instant the car struck a projection on the edge of the road and skidded onto the shoulder. Herbert grabbed the wheel. "Honey . . . !"

That's all I remember. Later I was told we slammed into a power pole. The impact loosened some transformers, causing them to plummet earthward, through the roof of the car onto Herbert, who died three hours later.

Words can't describe the devastation I felt. Nor the guilt. Day after day I brooded about the accident. Why had it happened? What could I have done to prevent it? I had counted on a happy marriage and now that hope was shattered. When rumors reached me that some people blamed me for the accident, I decided to go back to Patterson. There I found work in a bakery and, as always happens, time eventually healed my wounds. There I also found new direction for my life.

God spoke to me through a neighboring pastor who asked me to become the parish worker for his church.

"I am not qualified," I answered. "I must get training."

"Then get training."

"I can't. I have no money."

A decisive person, he said, "We will pray. In the meantime I will write to our church college and make arrangements for you to go there to study. I'm sure they will give you a 'special dispensation.' If they do, you can acquire high school credentials while you get your Bible training. Our church will help with finances."

My sister, Nellie, whose husband served in the United States Army overseas, also offered to help. "I will move in with Mom," she said.

When the president of our denomination and secretary of our world missions' board heard of my plans, they told me I was needed in Alaska.

Alaska? A stone's throw from Russia? Never!

But by the time I had completed my training, a rugged assignment for one with so little schooling, I had changed my mind. I did go to Alaska, first to work in village churches. On one assignment I lived in Golovan, 275 miles from the Russian mainland. Mother flew up to visit me and stayed for nearly three years. The Eskimos loved her. Short and stocky, with dark hair and eyes almost as black as theirs, she looked more Eskimo than American when she donned the parka and boots the village women made for her.

It was while Mother lived with me that we learned

what had happened to Tante Agnes, Mother's sister whose husband had disappeared after he was imprisoned, for leaving his home without permission. Her daughter-in-law wrote about the death of Grandfather and Grandmother Funk shortly after we had left for America, adding:

When Hitler became the ruler of Germany he demanded that all German citizens return to Germany. Since my father-in-law was a German citizen when he disappeared this meant my husband and his brother were considered German citizens, too. So the Russian government granted permission for us to go to Germany. Immediately the men were called into the army.

Those were dark, horrible days, Aunt Margaretha. The Russians captured the area where your sister, my mother-in-law, and I lived with my four children. Russian soldiers plundered our village . . . and raped! One night they tied Mother Agnes and me to tables and used us again and again. Before they left they shot all of the animals and left them where they lay. This worked to our good. We had meat to eat and to share.

But when that was gone I had to go into the fields and glean food for my family. Because I could not leave Mother alone (she was very frail) I put her in a wheelbarrow and took her into the fields with me.

One day God in his mercy called her home. I did not know what to do. I didn't have any shovel with me. I asked the children to help me and together, with our bare hands, we dug a grave and buried her.

Later I managed to escape, but five years passed before I was united with my husband. . . .

After Mother returned to the States, I became house mother in a Children's Home in White Mountain, Alaska. There I lost my heart to the lonely, problem-scarred children who came to the orphanage from broken homes or from homes where parents had died or abandoned them. I worked long hours, washed thousands of sheets, baked additional thousands of loaves of bread. Though I loved my work I longed to have someone share the job of parenting the children.

On furlough, I took my problem to God. Claiming John 5:7 I said, "Lord, the children need a father and I need a husband. Can't you find one for me?"

Preposterous? Perhaps. But God did provide a husband for me. I found him in Ashtabula, Ohio, on one of my furlough assignments. A linotype operator, a quiet, jack-of-all-trades individual, Jewel Matson joined me in Alaska.

Once I ventured to ask. "What did you think of me the first time you saw me?"

He chuckled. "I told my mother, 'She's too fat for me.' " I was and I am. Love for food is my thorn in the flesh born during those starvation days in Russia.

When people asked him how, during the long Alaskan winters, he managed to put up with a chatterbox, he'd answer, "I get a lot of fresh air."

One day after we had been married close to 17 years, our orphanage light plant caught on fire. Running back and forth to the water pump, lugging bucket after bucket of water up the knoll on which the plant stood, he suffered a heart attack and died.

I came back to the States a broken woman. Immediately pressured into furlough missionary speaking and other missionary assignments, I was forced to put aside thoughts that choked my soul. Several years passed before I mustered enough courage to go back to Alaska and sort through the things I had left in such haste. My brother, George, and his wife, Leah, accompanied me. I needed them.

I found myself on that trip. Coming home by way of Hawaii I spent a great deal of time in meditation and prayer. I also dipped into the writings of Aleksandr Solzhenitsyn. His book, *The Gulag Archipelago*, made my skin crawl. I wanted to join him and shout, "Wake up, America! Wake up!"

We all know that a great number of Soviet Jews wish to emigrate but are not permitted to do so. Few, however, are aware that nearly 6,000 dissatisfied Soviet Mennonites have applied for and been denied visas that would enable them to leave Russia. How thankful I am that our family escaped when we did.

In Hawaii I also came to realize as never before that though my life has had its share of sorrow it has had a much greater share of joy ... especially in serving God where he wanted me to be.

When he called me, I chose to be his servant. I

was free to do so, because I lived, not in Soviet Russia, but in the United States of America !